knitted farm animals

knitted farm animals

A collection of farmyard friends to knit from scratch

Sarah Keen

First published 2012 by
Guild of Master Craftsman Publications Ltd
Castle Place, 166 High Street, Lewes,
East Sussex BN7 1XU

Reprinted 2013, 2015

Illustrations by Simon Rodway, except for those on the right
of page 112 and on page 120.

ISBN 978-1-86108-846-8

Publisher: Jonathan Bailey
Production Manager: Jim Bulley
Managing Editor: Gerrie Purcell
Senior Project Editor: Dominique Page
Editor: Lorraine Slipper
Managing Art Editor: Gilda Pacitti
Designers: Rebecca Mothersole and Simon Goggin
Photographer: Rebecca Mothersole

Set in Frutiger
Colour origination by GMC Reprographics
Printed and bound in China

Dedicated to
Daniel, Samuel and Joshua

Where to find those friendly farmyard animals

Introduction

I have followed up my first book *Knitted Wild Animals* with a book of farmyard animals. It's been very exciting creating the designs for this book and I began with the obvious animals – cow, sheep, pig – then added some more unusual ones, such as the llama, Highland bull and turkey, making a collection of 15.

Each of the animals has clear making-up instructions together with beautiful photographs of the toys, which will ensure that the final touches to each animal are easily made.

I have enjoyed creating these animals and hope that you too will find pleasure in whichever animals you decide to make.

Sarah Keen

COW >> 42

LLAMA >> 102

DONKEY >> 106

ROOSTER >> 64

CHICK >>
58

58 << CHICK

CHICK >>

58

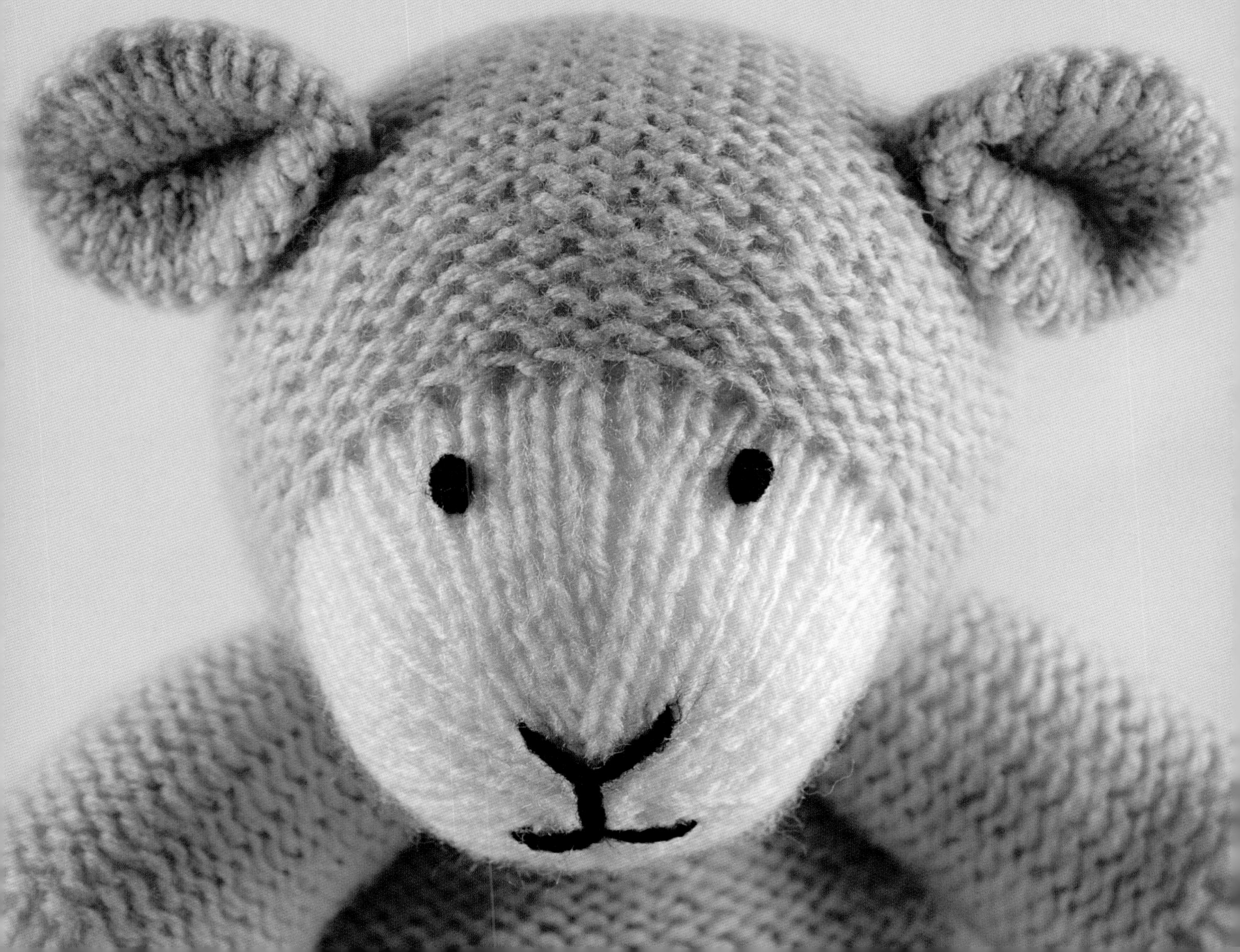

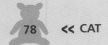

DUCKLINGS >> 70

DUCKLING >>
70

DUCKLING >>
70

HEN >> 58

CHICK >> 58

CHICK >> 58

58 << EGG

58 << HEN

CHICK >>
58

58 << EGG

CHICK >> 58

Affectionate donkey

Beady-eyed rooster

Clever pig

Adventurous goat

Sociable llama

The farm animals

The average cow produces about 2,768 gal (10,478 l) of milk each year, more when listening to classical music. Back in 1930s America, an unusually productive dairy cow, Elm Farm Ollie, took to the skies in an aeroplane as part of a publicity stunt. In what may very well be the first, if not the only, case of air delivery, the containers of milk were attached to small parachutes and dropped from the plane as it flew over the city of St Louis in Missouri.

COW

DID YOU KNOW?
Cows are incapable of walking downstairs because of the way their legs bend.

Information you'll need

Finished size
Cow measures 10in (25cm) in height

Materials
Any DK yarn:
80g white (A)
20g biscuit (B)
30g black (C)
5g beige (D)
Oddment of grey for features
Note: amounts are generous
but approximate
A pair of 3.25mm (US3:UK10) needles
Acrylic toy stuffing
Knitters' blunt-ended pins and a knitters'
needle for sewing up
Tweezers for stuffing small parts (optional)

Tension
26 sts x 34 rows measure 4in (10cm)
square over stocking-st using 3.25mm
needles and DK yarn before stuffing

Abbreviations
See page 123

How to make Cow

Body (make 2 pieces)

Beg at lower edge using the thumb method and A, cast on 35 sts.

First and foll 4 alt rows (WS): Purl.

Inc row: K10, m1, k15, m1, k10 (37 sts).

Inc row: K11, m1, k15, m1, k11 (39 sts).

Inc row: K12, m1, k15, m1, k12 (41 sts).

Inc row: K13, m1, k15, m1, k13 (43 sts).

Inc row: K14, m1, k15, m1, k14 (45 sts).

Beg with a purl row, stocking-st 11 rows.

Shape sides

Dec row: K2tog, k to last 2 sts, k2tog tbl.

Next row: Purl.

Rep last 2 rows 12 times more (19 sts).

Cast off.

Base

Using the thumb method and A, cast on 20 sts.

First row (WS): Purl.

Inc row: K1, m1, k to last st, m1, k1.

Rep first 2 rows 5 times more (32 sts).

Beg with a purl row, stocking-st 5 rows.

Dec row: K2tog, k to last 2 sts, k2tog tbl.

Next row: Purl.

Rep last 2 rows 5 times more (20 sts).

Cast off.

Head

Beg at centre of underneath side using the thumb method and A, cast on 30 sts. Place a marker at centre of cast-on edge.

First and foll alt row (WS): Purl.

Inc row: K4, (m1, k2) 4 times, k8, (m1, k2) 4 times, k2 (38 sts).

Inc row: K6, (m1, k2) 4 times, k12, (m1, k2) 4 times, k4 (46 sts).

Beg with a purl row, stocking-st 21 rows.

Dec row: K10, (k2tog) twice, k18, (k2tog) twice, k10 (42 sts).

Next and foll 3 alt rows: Purl.

Dec row: K9, (k2tog) twice, k16, (k2tog) twice, k9 (38 sts).

Dec row: K8, (k2tog) twice, k14, (k2tog) twice, k8 (34 sts).

Dec row: K7, (k2tog) twice, k12, (k2tog) twice, k7 (30 sts).

Dec row: (K2tog) to end (15 sts).

Purl 1 row.

Thread yarn through sts on needle, pull tight and secure.

Muzzle

Using the thumb method and B, cast on 24 sts.

Place a marker at centre of cast-on edge.

First and foll alt row (WS): Purl.

Inc row: K2, (m1, k2) 5 times, k2, (m1, k2) 5 times (34 sts).

Inc row: K4, (m1, k3) 4 times, k5, (m1, k3) 4 times, k1 (42 sts).

Beg with a purl row, stocking-st 5 rows.

Dec row: K7, (k2tog, k1) 3 times, k11, (k2tog, k1) 3 times, k6 (36 sts).

Purl 1 row.

Cast off.

COW

Lower body patch

Using the thumb method and C, cast on 6 sts and work in garter-st.

Rows 1, 3, 5 and 7 (RS): Knit.

Rows 2, 4 and 6: (K1, m1) twice, k to last st, m1, k1.

Rows 8, 10, 12, 14 and 16: K to last 2 sts, (m1, k1) twice.

Rows 9, 11, 13 and 15: Knit.

Rows 17 to 28: Garter-st 12 rows (25 sts).

Rows 29 and 31: K to last 2 sts, k2tog.

Row 30: Knit.

Rows 32 to 47: Garter-st 16 rows (23 sts).

Row 48: K1, m1, k to end (24 sts).

Rows 49 to 60: Garter-st 12 rows.

Rows 61, 63, 65, 67, 69 and 71: K to last 2 sts, k2tog.

Rows 62, 64, 66, 68, 70 and 72: Knit.

Rows 73 to 78: Garter-st 6 rows (18 sts).

Rows 79, 81, 83, 85 and 87: K2tog, k to last 2 sts, k2tog.

Rows 80, 82, 84, 86 and 88: Knit.

Row 89: (K2tog) to end (4 sts).
Cast off.

Upper body patch

Using the thumb method and C, cast on 6 sts and work in garter-st.

Rows 1, 3 and 5 (RS): Knit.

Rows 2, 4 and 6: K1, m1, k to last st, m1, k1.

Rows 7 to 11: Garter-st 5 rows (12 sts).

Rows 12, 14 and 16: K to last 2 sts, (m1, k1) twice.

Rows 13 and 15: Knit.

Rows 17 to 24: Garter-st 8 rows (18 sts).

Rows 25, 27 and 29: K to last 2 sts, k2tog.

Rows 26 and 28: Knit.

Rows 30 to 44: Garter-st 15 rows (15 sts).

Rows 45, 47 and 49: K2tog, k to end.

Rows 46 and 48: Knit.

Rows 50 to 54: Garter-st 5 rows (12 sts).

Rows 55 and 57: K2tog, k to last 2 sts, k2tog.

Rows 56 and 58: Knit.

Row 59: (K2tog) to end (4 sts).
Cast off.

DID YOU KNOW?

Every day cows eat about 40lb (18kg) of food and drink enough water to fill a bath tub!

Head patch

Using the thumb method and C, cast on 6 sts and work in garter-st.

Rows 1, 3 and 5 (RS): Knit.

Rows 2 and 4: (K1, m1) twice, k to last 2 sts, (m1, k1) twice.

Rows 6, 8, 10 and 12: K to last st, m1, k1.

Rows 7, 9 and 11: Knit.

Rows 13 to 32: Garter-st 20 rows (18 sts).

Row 33: K2tog, k to last 2 sts, k2tog (16 sts).

Row 34: Knit.

Rows 35 and 37: (K2tog) twice, k to last 4 sts, (k2tog) twice.

Rows 36 and 38: Knit.

Row 39: (K2tog) to end (4 sts).

Cast off.

Hind legs (make 2)

Beg at hoof using the thumb method and C, cast on 18 sts.

Purl 1 row.

Inc row (RS): K2, (m1, k2) to end (26 sts).

Beg with a purl row, stocking-st 9 rows.

Change to A and dec.

Dec row: K2, (k2tog, k2) to end (20 sts).

Beg with a purl row, stocking-st 3 rows.

Inc row: (K2, m1) twice, k12, (m1, k2) twice (24 sts).

Next and foll alt row: Purl.

Inc row: (K2, m1) twice, k16, (m1, k2) twice (28 sts).

Inc row: (K2, m1) twice, k20, (m1, k2) twice (32 sts).

Beg with a purl row, stocking-st 11 rows.

Cast off.

Forelegs (make 2)

Beg at hoof using the thumb method and A, cast on 14 sts.

Purl 1 row.

Inc row: K2, (m1, k2) to end (20 sts).

Beg with a purl row, stocking-st 7 rows.

Change to C and dec.

Dec row: (K2, k2tog) to end (15 sts).

Beg with a purl row, stocking-st 3 rows.

Inc row: K3, (m1, k3) to end (19 sts).

Beg with a purl row, stocking-st 5 rows.

Inc row: K7, m1, k5, m1, k7 (21 sts).

Beg with a purl row, stocking-st 3 rows.

Inc row: K8, m1, k5, m1, k8 (23 sts).

Beg with a purl row, stocking-st 13 rows.

Dec row: K2tog, (k1, k2tog) to end (15 sts).

Purl 1 row.

Thread yarn through sts on needle, pull tight and secure.

Horns (make 2)

Beg at lower edge using the thumb method and D, cast on 10 sts.

Beg with a purl row, stocking-st 3 rows.

Dec row: (K2tog, k3) twice (8 sts).

Beg with a purl row, stocking-st 3 rows.

Dec row: (K2tog, k2) twice (6 sts).

Purl 1 row.

Thread yarn through sts on needle, pull tight and secure.

Ears (make 2)

Using the thumb method and C, cast on 20 sts and work in garter-st.

Garter-st 2 rows.

Dec row: K4, k2tog, k2, (k2tog) twice, k2, k2tog, k4 (16 sts).

Knit 1 row.

Dec row: K5, (k3tog) twice, k5 (12 sts).

Cast off in garter-st.

DID YOU KNOW?

A Holstein's spots are like fingerprints or snowflakes: entirely unique. No two cows have exactly the same pattern of spots.

COW

47

Making up

Body

Place the two halves of the body together matching all edges and join row ends. Stuff body leaving neck and lower edge open, filling out base with plenty of stuffing.

Base

Pin base to lower edge of body and sew base to body leaving a gap. Adjust stuffing in base, adding more stuffing if needed, and close gap.

Head

Join row ends of head and stuff. Bring seam and marker together and oversew cast-on stitches. Pin and sew head to body, adding more stuffing to body if needed.

Muzzle

Join row ends of muzzle. Bring seam and marker together and join cast-on stitches. Stuff muzzle, leaving cast-off stitches open. Pin and sew muzzle to head.

Patches

Pin and sew patches to body and head using backstitch, all the way round outside edge of patches.

Hind legs

Join row ends of hooves and, with seam at centre of underneath side, join cast-on stitches. Join row ends of hind legs. Place a ball of stuffing into each hoof and stuff legs. Place body on a flat surface and pin hind legs to body. Sew cast-off stitches of hind legs to body all the way round.

Forelegs

Fold cast-on stitches of forelegs in half and join. Join row ends of forelegs, leaving a gap, and place a small ball of stuffing into each hoof. Stuff forelegs and close gap. Sew forelegs to body at shoulders.

Horns

Join row ends of horns and stuff, pushing stuffing in with tweezers or tip of scissors. To curl horns, sew a running stitch along seam, pull tight and secure. Sew cast-on stitches of horns to head all the way round.

Ears

Fold cast-off stitches of ears in half and oversew together. Fold row ends of each ear in half and oversew, and sew ears to head at each side below horns.

Tail

Make a twisted cord out of 8 strands of A, each piece 30in (75cm) long (see page 120). Tie a knot 2½in (6cm) from folded end and trim ends beyond knot to 1in (2.5cm). Sew folded end of tail to Cow at back.

Features

To make eyes, tie 2 knots in 2 lengths of grey yarn, winding the yarn round 6 times to make each knot (see page 120). Tie eyes to head and run ends into head. Work nostrils in the same way using C and tie to muzzle, running ends into muzzle.

Sheep are intelligent beings. They can remember up to 50 other sheep faces and have even been shown to have problem-solving abilities. One flock discovered a way to get over cattle grids by rolling across on their backs! Sheep can often be found in unusual places – they have even been discovered on the roofs of houses! They have also been known to graze on the White House lawn to keep it neat and well trimmed.

EWE

DID YOU KNOW?

A lamb can identify its mother by her bleat.

Information you'll need

Finished size
Ewe measures 8½in (21.5cm) in height

Materials
Any DK yarn:
80g oatmeal (A)
30g cream (B)
Oddment of black for features
Note: amounts are generous
but approximate
A pair of 3.25mm (US3:UK10) needles
Acrylic toy stuffing
Knitters' blunt-ended pins and a knitters'
needle for sewing up

Tension
26 sts x 34 rows measure 4in (10cm)
square over rev stocking-st using 3.25mm
needles and DK yarn before stuffing

Abbreviations
See page 123

ewe

How to make Ewe

Body (make 2 pieces)

Beg at lower edge using the thumb method and A, cast on 32 sts and work in rev stocking-st.

First and foll 3 alt rows (RS): Purl.
Inc row: K9, m1, k14, m1, k9 (34 sts).
Inc row: K10, m1, k14, m1, k10 (36 sts).
Inc row: K11, m1, k14, m1, k11 (38 sts).
Inc row: K12, m1, k14, m1, k12 (40 sts).
Beg with a purl row, rev stocking-st 11 rows.

Shape sides
Dec row: K2tog, k to last 2 sts, k2tog tbl.
Next row: Purl.
Rep last 2 rows 11 times more (16 sts).
Cast off.

Base

Using the thumb method and A, cast on 16 sts and work in rev stocking-st.
First row (RS): Purl.
Inc row: K1, m1, k to last st, m1, k1.
Rep these 2 rows 4 times more (26 sts).
Beg with a purl row, rev stocking-st 5 rows.
Dec row: K2tog, k to last 2 sts, k2tog tbl.
Next row: Purl.
Rep last 2 rows 4 times more (16 sts).
Cast off.

Head

Beg at centre back of head using the thumb method and A, cast on 9 sts and beg in rev stocking-st.
First and foll 5 alt rows (RS): Purl.
Inc row: K1, (m1, k1) to end (17 sts).
Inc row: K1, (m1, k2) to end (25 sts).

Inc row: K1, (m1, k3) to end (33 sts).
Inc row: K1, (m1, k4) to end (41 sts).
Inc row: K1, (m1, k5) to end (49 sts).
Inc row: K1, (m1, k6) to end (57 sts).
Beg with a purl row, rev stocking-st 13 rows.
Dec row: K5, (k2tog, k1) 16 times, k4 (41 sts).
Beg with a purl row, rev stocking-st 3 rows.
Dec row: K7, (k2tog, k3) 6 times, k4 (35 sts).
Change to B and cont in stocking-st.
Next row: (K1tbl) to end.
Beg with a purl row, stocking-st 3 rows.
Dec row: (K3, k2tog) to end (28 sts).
Beg with a purl row, stocking-st 5 rows.
Dec row: (K2, k2tog) to end (21 sts).
Next and foll alt row: Purl.
Dec row: (K1, k2tog) to end (14 sts).
Dec row: (K2tog) to end (7 sts).
Thread yarn through sts on needle, pull tight and secure.

Hind legs (make 2)

Using the thumb method and A, cast on 27 sts and beg in rev stocking-st.
Beg with a purl row, rev stocking-st 11 rows.
Change to B and cont in stocking-st and beg with a purl row, stocking-st 7 rows.
Dec row: (K1, k2tog) to end (18 sts).
Purl 1 row.
Dec row: (K2tog) to end (9 sts).
Thread yarn through sts on needle, pull tight and secure.

Forelegs (make 2)

Using the thumb method and A, cast on 20 sts and beg in rev stocking-st.
Beg with a purl row, rev stocking-st 19 rows.
Change to B and cont in stocking-st and beg with a purl row, stocking-st 7 rows.
Dec row: (K2tog) to end (10 sts).
Thread yarn through sts on needle, pull tight and secure.

Ears (make 2)

Using the thumb method and A, cast on 12 sts and beg in stocking-st.
First and foll alt row (WS): Purl.
Inc row: K2, (m1, k2) to end (17 sts).
Inc row: K7, (m1, k1) 4 times, k6 (21 sts).
Beg with a purl row, stocking-st 2 rows ending on a knit row.
Cont in rev stocking-st and beg with a knit row, stocking-st 2 rows.
Dec row: K5, (k2tog, k1) 4 times, k4 (17 sts).
Purl 1 row.
Dec row: K2, (k2tog) 3 times, k1, (k2tog) 3 times, k2 (11 sts).
Cast off p-wise.

Tail

Beg at base using the thumb method and A, cast on 14 sts and work in rev stocking-st.
Beg with a purl row, rev stocking-st 21 rows.
Dec row: (K2tog) to end (7 sts).
Thread yarn through sts on needle, pull tight and secure.

Making up

Body

With reverse side of stocking stitch as the right side, place the two halves of the body together matching all edges and join row ends. Stuff body leaving neck and lower edge open, filling out base with plenty of stuffing.

Base

Pin base to lower edge of body, noting that the reverse side of stocking stitch is the right side and sew base to body leaving a gap. Adjust stuffing in base, adding more stuffing if needed, and close gap.

Head

Gather round cast-on stitches of head, pull tight and secure. Join row ends of head leaving a gap, stuff head, pushing stuffing into snout and top of head. Close gap and pin and sew head to body, adding more stuffing to body if needed.

Hind legs

Join row ends of hind legs and stuff. Place body on a flat surface and pin hind legs to body. Sew cast-on stitches of hind legs to body all the way round.

Forelegs

Join row ends of forelegs and stuff. With seam at centre of inside edge, oversew cast-on stitches. Sew forelegs to each side of body, sewing cast-on stitches to neck.

Ears

Join cast-on and cast-off stitches of ears. Fold this seam in half and oversew. Fold ears in half and catch row ends in place, and sew ears to head at each side.

Tail

With reverse of stocking stitch as the right side, join row ends of tail, place 2 tiny balls of stuffing into tail and sew tail to back of Ewe.

Features

To make eyes, tie 2 knots in 2 lengths of black yarn, winding the yarn round 6 times to make each knot (see page 120). Tie eyes to head with 5 clear knitted stitches in between and run ends into head. Embroider nose in black using straight stitches as shown in picture (see page 120 for how to begin and fasten off invisibly for the embroidery).

Pigs are very clever and learn quickly. Piglets, for example, learn their names by three weeks old and will respond when called. They are very social animals that form close bonds with each other and will lie close together when resting. They also enjoy rolling around in the mud together to cool their skin and to protect themselves from the sun – they're susceptible to sunburn, particularly those with pale skin!

PIG

DID YOU KNOW?
If a pig were able to fly, other pigs would be unable to see him, as it is physically impossible for a pig to look up.

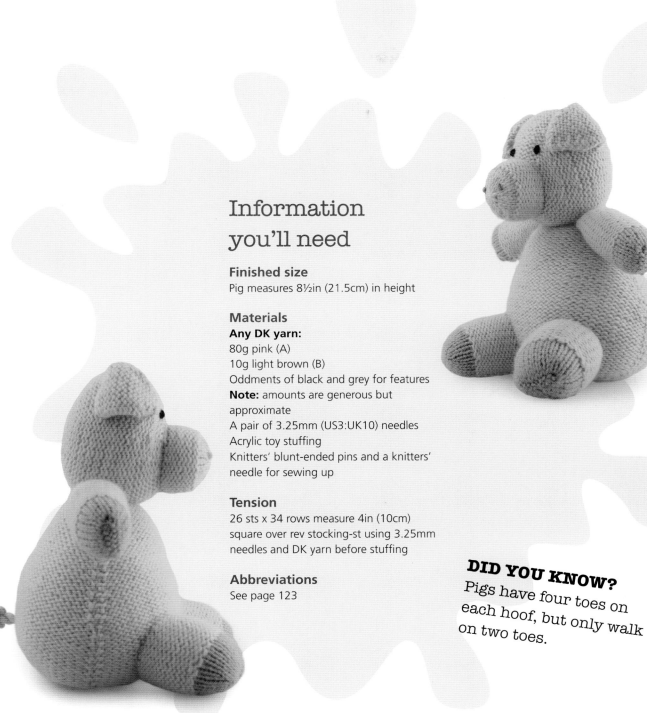

Information you'll need

Finished size
Pig measures 8½in (21.5cm) in height

Materials
Any DK yarn:
80g pink (A)
10g light brown (B)
Oddments of black and grey for features
Note: amounts are generous but
approximate
A pair of 3.25mm (US3:UK10) needles
Acrylic toy stuffing
Knitters' blunt-ended pins and a knitters'
needle for sewing up

Tension
26 sts x 34 rows measure 4in (10cm)
square over rev stocking-st using 3.25mm
needles and DK yarn before stuffing

Abbreviations
See page 123

DID YOU KNOW?
Pigs have four toes on
each hoof, but only walk
on two toes.

How to make Pig

Body back

Beg at lower edge using the thumb method and A, cast on 32 sts and work in rev stocking-st.

First and foll 3 alt rows (RS): Purl.
Inc row: K9, m1, k14, m1, k9 (34 sts).
Inc row: K10, m1, k14, m1, k10 (36 sts).
Inc row: K11, m1, k14, m1, k11 (38 sts).
Inc row: K12, m1, k14, m1, k12 (40 sts).
Purl 1 row.

Work hole to attach tail
Next row: K19, cast off next 2 sts, k to end (38 sts).
Next row: P19 sts, using the cable method cast on 2 sts, p to end (40 sts).
Beg with a knit row, rev stocking-st 8 rows.

Shape sides
Dec row: K2tog, k to last 2 sts, k2tog tbl.
Next row: Purl.
Rep last 2 rows 11 times more (16 sts).
Cast off.

Body front

Work as for body back omitting hole for tail (rev stocking-st these 2 rows).

Base

Using the thumb method and A, cast on 16 sts and work in rev stocking-st.
First row (RS): Purl.
Inc row: K1, m1, k to last st, m1, k1.
Rep first 2 rows 4 times more (26 sts).
Beg with a purl row, rev stocking-st 5 rows.
Dec row: K2tog, k to last 2 sts, k2tog tbl.
Next row: Purl.
Rep last 2 rows 4 times more (16 sts).
Cast off.

Head

Beg at centre back of head using the thumb method and A, cast on 9 sts and work in rev stocking-st.
First and foll 5 alt rows (RS): Purl.
Inc row: K1, (m1, k1) to end (17 sts).
Inc row: K1, (m1, k2) to end (25 sts).
Inc row: K1, (m1, k3) to end (33 sts).
Inc row: K1, (m1, k4) to end (41 sts).
Inc row: K1, (m1, k5) to end (49 sts).
Inc row: K1, (m1, k6) to end (57 sts).
Beg with a purl row, rev stocking-st 13 rows.
Dec row: K11, (k2tog, k1) 12 times, k10 (45 sts).
Beg with a purl row, rev stocking-st 3 rows.
Dec row: K8, (k2tog, k1) 10 times, k7 (35 sts).
Beg with a purl row, stocking-st 3 rows.
Dec row: (K3, k2tog) to end (28 sts).
Next and foll 2 alt rows: Purl.
Dec row: (K2, k2tog) to end (21 sts).
Dec row: (K1, k2tog) to end (14 sts).
Dec row: (K2tog) to end (7 sts).
Thread yarn through sts on needle, pull tight and secure.

Snout

Using the thumb method and A, cast on 24 sts and beg in rev stocking-st.
Beg with a purl row, rev stocking-st 9 rows.
Cont in stocking-st and beg with a purl row, stocking-st 3 rows.
Dec row: (K2tog, k1) to end (16 sts).
Purl 1 row.
Dec row: (K2tog) to end (8 sts).
Thread yarn through sts on needle, pull tight and secure.

Hind legs (make 2)

Using the thumb method and A, cast on 28 sts and beg in rev stocking-st.
Beg with a purl row, rev stocking-st 13 rows.
Dec row: (K4, k2tog, k2, k2tog, k4) twice (24 sts).
Change to B, cont in stocking-st and beg with a knit row, stocking-st 6 rows.
Dec row: (K3, k2tog, k2, k2tog, k3) twice (20 sts).
Purl 1 row.
Cast off.

Forelegs (make 2)

Using the thumb method and A, cast on 20 sts and beg in rev stocking-st.
Beg with a purl row, rev stocking-st 20 rows, ending on a knit row.
Change to B, cont in stocking-st and beg with a knit row, stocking-st 4 rows.
Dec row: (K1, k2tog, k4, k2tog, k1) twice (16 sts).
Purl 1 row.
Cast off.

Ears (make 2)

Beg at base edge using the thumb method and A, cast on 20 sts and work in rev stocking-st.
Beg with a purl row, rev stocking-st 11 rows.
Dec row: *K3, (k2tog) twice, k3; rep from * once (16 sts).
Next and foll 2 alt rows: Purl.
Dec row: *K2, (k2tog) twice, k2; rep from * once (12 sts).
Dec row: *K1, (k2tog) twice, k1; rep from * once (8 sts).
Dec row: (K2tog) to end (4 sts).
Thread yarn through sts on needle, pull tight and secure.

Making up

Tail

Make a twisted cord out of 6 strands of A, each piece 32in (80cm) long (see page 120). Tie a tight knot 3½in (9cm) from folded end and tie another knot for external tail at folded end. Trim ends beyond tight knot to ½in (1cm). Using A, gather round hole in back of body of pig, insert tail and sew in place securely, noting that the reverse side of stocking stitch is the right side.

Body

With reverse stocking stitch as the right side, place the two halves of the body together, matching all edges, and join row ends. Stuff body leaving neck and lower edge open, filling out base with plenty of stuffing.

Base

Pin base to lower edge of body, noting that the reverse side of stocking stitch is the right side and sew base to body leaving a gap. Adjust stuffing in base, adding more stuffing if needed, and close the gap.

Head and snout

Gather round cast-on stitches of head, pull tight and secure. Join row ends of head leaving a gap, stuff head and close gap. Join row ends of snout and stuff. Sew cast-on edge of snout to lower half of head all the way round. Pin and sew head to body, adding more stuffing to body if needed.

Hind legs

Join row ends of hind legs and with this seam at centre of underneath side of leg, oversew cast-off stitches and stuff. Place body on a flat surface and pin hind legs to body. Sew cast-on stitches of legs to body all the way round.

Forelegs

Fold cast-off stitches in half and oversew. Join row ends and stuff forelegs. With this seam at centre of inside edge, join cast-on stitches. Sew forelegs to each side of body sewing cast-on stitches to neck.

Ears

With reverse side of stocking stitch as the right side, join row ends of ears. With this seam at centre of inside edge, oversew cast-on stitches and sew cast-on stitches of ears to each side of head. Curl ears forwards and catch in place.

Features

To make eyes, tie 2 knots in 2 lengths of black yarn, winding the yarn round 6 times to make each knot (see page 120). Tie eyes to head above snout and run ends into head. Make 2 nostrils in grey in the same way as the eyes, winding the yarn round 4 times to make the knots. Tie nostrils to snout and run ends in.

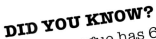
DID YOU KNOW?
A pig's tongue has 6,000 more taste buds than a human's.

The average hen lays 227 eggs a year. The colour of her first egg is the colour she will lay for life. Hens that lay brown eggs have brownish red feathers and ear lobes. White eggs come from hens with white feathers and white ear lobes. Astonishingly, hens can even lay green, pink and blue eggs. They will produce larger eggs as they grow older. The largest hen egg ever laid weighed 1lb (almost 0.5kg) and had a double yolk and shell.

HEN, CHICKS AND EGGS

DID YOU KNOW?
The chicken is the closest living relative of the T-rex!

Information you'll need

Finished sizes
Hen measures 6in (15cm) in height
Chicks measure 2½in (6cm) in height
Eggs measure 2½in (6cm) in length

Materials
Any DK yarn:
50g ginger (A)
20g yellow (B)
20g red (C)
20g lemon (D)
10g orange (E)
10g light brown (F)
Oddment of black for features
Note: amounts are generous
but approximate
A pair of 3.25mm (US3:UK10)
knitting needles
Acrylic toy stuffing
Knitters' blunt-ended pins and a knitters'
needle for sewing up
Tweezers for stuffing small parts (optional)

Tension
26 sts x 34 rows measure 4in (10cm)
square over stocking-st using 3.25mm
needles and DK yarn before stuffing

Abbreviations
See page 123

hen, chicks and eggs

How to make Hen

Body and head

Beg at lower edge using the thumb method and A, cast on 24 sts.

First and foll 10 alt rows (WS): Purl.

Inc row: *(K1, m1) twice, k8, (m1, k1) twice; rep from * once (32 sts).

Inc row: (K1, m1, k14, m1, k1) twice (36 sts).

Inc row: (K1, m1, k16, m1, k1) twice (40 sts).

Inc row: (K1, m1, k18, m1, k1) twice (44 sts).

Inc row: (K1, m1, k20, m1, k1) twice (48 sts).

Inc row: (K1, m1, k22, m1, k1) twice (52 sts).

Inc row: (K1, m1, k24, m1, k1) twice (56 sts).

Inc row: (K1, m1, k26, m1, k1) twice (60 sts).

Inc row: (K1, m1, k28, m1, k1) twice (64 sts).

Inc row: (K1, m1, k30, m1, k1) twice (68 sts).

Inc row: (K1, m1, k32, m1, k1) twice (72 sts).

Next row: Purl.

Inc row: K1, m1, k to last st, m1, k1. Rep last 2 rows once (76 sts).

Beg with a purl row, stocking-st 3 rows.

Inc row: K1, m1, k to last st, m1, k1 (78 sts).

Beg with a purl row, stocking-st 3 rows.

Shape neck

Row 1: K36, turn.
Row 2: S1p, p to end.
Row 3: K33, turn.
Row 4: S1p, p to end.
Row 5: K30, turn.
Row 6: S1p, p to end.

Shape tail

Row 1: K10, turn.
Row 2: S1p, p to end.

Row 3: K2tog, k6, turn (77 sts).
Row 4: S1p, p to end.
Row 5: K2tog, k3, turn (76 sts).
Row 6: S1p, p to end.
Cast off 21 sts at beg of next row (55 sts).

Shape second half of neck

Row 1: P36, turn.
Row 2: S1k, k to end.
Row 3: P33, turn.
Row 4: S1k, k to end.
Row 5: P30, turn.
Row 6: S1k, k to end.

Shape second half of tail

Row 1: P10, turn.
Row 2: S1k, k to end.
Row 3: P2tog, p6, turn (54 sts).
Row 4: S1k, k to end.
Row 5: P2tog, p3, turn (53 sts).
Row 6: S1k, k to end.
Cast off 21 sts p-wise at beg of next row (32 sts).
Stocking-st 12 rows.

Shape top of head

Dec row: (K2, k2tog) to end (24 sts).
Next and foll alt row: Purl.
Dec row: (K1, k2tog) to end (16 sts).
Dec row: (K2tog) to end (8 sts).
Thread yarn through sts on needle, pull tight and secure.

Feet (make 4 pieces)

Using the thumb method and B, cast on 8 sts.
Purl 1 row.

Inc row (RS): K1, (m1, k2) to last st, m1, k1 (12 sts).

Beg with a purl row, stocking-st 3 rows.

**Shape toes

Next row: K4, turn and work on these 4 sts.

Beg with a purl row, stocking-st 3 rows.

Dec row: K1, k2tog, k1 (3 sts).

Thread yarn through rem sts, pull tight and secure.**

With RS facing, rejoin yarn to sts on needle and rep from ** to ** twice.

Comb (make 2 pieces)

Begin at lower edge using the thumb method and C, cast on 12 sts.
Purl 1 row.

Inc row (RS): K1, (m1, k2) to last st, m1, k1 (18 sts).

**Shape comb

Next row: P6, turn and work on these 6 sts.

Beg with a knit row, stocking-st 2 rows.

Dec row: K2tog, k2, k2tog (4 sts).

Thread yarn through rem sts, pull tight and secure.**

With WS facing, rejoin yarn to sts on needle and rep from ** to ** twice.

Beak

Using the thumb method and B, cast on 8 sts.

Beg with a purl row, stocking-st 2 rows, ending on a knit row.

Dec row: (P2tog) to end (4 sts).

Thread yarn through sts on needle, pull tight and secure.

Crop (make 2)
Begin at top edge using the thumb method and C, cast on 3 sts.
First and foll alt row (WS): Purl.
Inc row: K1, m1, k1, m1, k1 (5 sts).
Inc row: K2, m1, k1, m1, k2 (7 sts).
Beg with a purl row, stocking-st 3 rows.
Dec row: K1, k2tog, k1, k2tog, k1 (5 sts).
Thread yarn through sts on needle, pull tight and secure.

Eye pieces (make 2)
Using the thumb method and C, cast on 6 sts.
First and foll 2 alt rows (WS): Purl.
Inc row: K1, m1, k4, m1, k1 (8 sts).
Shape next row: K1, m1, (k2tog) 3 times, m1, k1 (7 sts).
Dec row: K2tog, k3, k2tog (5 sts).
Dec row: P1, p3tog, p1 (3 sts).
Thread yarn through sts on needle, pull tight and secure.

Wings (make 2)
Using the thumb method and A, cast on 12 sts.
First and foll 2 alt rows (WS): Purl.
Inc row: *(K1, m1) twice, k2, (m1, k1) twice; rep from * once (20 sts).
Inc row: (K1, m1, k8, m1, k1) twice (24 sts).
Inc row: (K1, m1, k10, m1, k1) twice (28 sts).
Beg with a purl row, stocking-st 9 rows.
Dec row: (K2tog, k10, k2tog) twice (24 sts).
Next and foll 3 alt rows: Purl.
Dec row: (K2tog, k8, k2tog) twice (20 sts).
Dec row: (K2tog, k6, k2tog) twice (16 sts).
Dec row: (K2tog, k4, k2tog) twice (12 sts).
Dec row: (K2tog) to end (6 sts).
Thread yarn through sts on needle, pull tight and secure.

Making up
Body and head
Join row ends of head and body and join cast-off stitches at back. Stuff body, pushing stuffing into head and tail. Fold cast-on stitches in half and oversew.

Feet
Place 2 pieces of feet together matching all edges and oversew on right side around toes. Stuff toes, pushing stuffing into toes with tweezers or tip of scissors. Stuff feet and join cast-on stitches. Place Hen on a flat surface and pin feet to body. Sew in place.

Comb
Place 2 pieces of comb together matching all edges and oversew on right side around shaped row ends. Stuff comb, pushing stuffing in with tweezers or tip of scissors. Join cast-on stitches and pin and sew comb to top of head all the way round lower edge.

Beak
Join row ends of beak and stuff with a tiny ball of stuffing, pushing stuffing in with tweezers or tip of scissors. Sew beak to head all the way round.

Crop
Join row ends of lower half of each piece of crop and stuff lower half with a tiny ball of stuffing, pushing stuffing in with tweezers or tip of scissors. Finish by joining row ends of both pieces, place them side by side and sew together. Sew crop to Hen below beak at centre front.

Eye pieces
Sew eye pieces to head using backstitch around outside edge.

Wings
Fold cast-on stitches of wings in half and oversew. Join row ends of wings on right side and pin and sew to sides of Hen, all the way round outer edge.

Features
To make eyes, tie 2 knots in 2 lengths of black yarn, winding the yarn round 6 times to make each knot (see page 120). Tie eyes to eye pieces and run ends into head.

How to make Chicks

Body

Beg at lower edge using the thumb method and D, cast on 6 sts and work in rev stocking-st.

First and foll 3 alt rows (RS): Purl.
Inc row: (Inc 1) to end (12 sts).
Inc row: (Inc 1, k1) to end (18 sts).
Inc row: (Inc 1, k2) to end (24 sts).
Inc row: (Inc 1, k3) to end (30 sts).
Beg with a purl row, rev stocking-st 7 rows.
Dec row: (K2tog, k3) to end (24 sts).
Next and foll 2 alt rows: Purl.
Dec row: (K2tog, k2) to end (18 sts).
Dec row: (K2tog, k1) to end (12 sts).
Dec row: (K2tog) to end (6 sts).
Thread yarn through sts on needle, pull tight and secure.

Head

Using the thumb method and D, cast on 20 sts and work in rev stocking-st. Beg with a purl row, rev stocking-st 5 rows.
Dec row (WS): (K2tog, k2) to end (15 sts).
Next and foll alt row: Purl.
Dec row: (K2tog, k1) to end (10 sts).
Dec row: (K2tog) to end (5 sts).
Thread yarn through sts on needle, pull tight and secure.

Feet (make 2)

Using the thumb method and E, cast on 3 sts and work in garter-st.
Garter-st 5 rows.
Cast off.

Beak

Using the thumb method and E, cast on 5 sts.
Thread yarn through these 5 sts, pull tight and secure.

Wings (make 2)

Using the thumb method and D, cast on 3 sts and work in rev stocking-st.
Purl 1 row.
Inc row (WS): K1, m1, k1, m1, k1 (5 sts).
Beg with a purl row, rev stocking-st 5 rows.
Dec row: K2tog, k1, k2tog tbl (3 sts).
Purl 1 row.
Cast off k-wise.

Making up

Body

With the reverse side of stocking stitch outside, gather round cast-on stitches of body, pull tight and secure. Join row ends of body leaving a gap. Stuff and close gap.

Head

With the reverse side of stocking stitch outside, join row ends of head. Place a ball of stuffing inside head and sew cast-on stitches of head to body all the way round.

Feet

Fold each foot and join cast-on and cast-off stitches. Place Chick on a flat surface and pin seams of feet to body with an approx 1in (2.5cm) gap in between. Sew seams of feet to Chick.

Beak

Join row ends of cast-on edge of beak. Sew beak to centre front of head.

Wings

With reverse side of stocking stitch outside, fold each wing in half, bringing cast-on and cast-off stitches together and join. Place wings either side of Chick and sew across top edge of each wing to body.

Features

To make eyes, tie 2 knots in 2 lengths of black yarn, winding the yarn round 3 times to make each knot (see page 120). Tie eyes to head and run ends into head.

How to make Eggs

Using the thumb method and F, cast on 5 sts.

First and foll 4 alt rows (WS): Purl.
Inc row: K1, (m1, k1) to end (9 sts).
Inc row: K1, (m1, k2) to end (13 sts).
Inc row: K1, (m1, k3) to end (17 sts).
Inc row: K1, (m1, k4) to end (21 sts).
Inc row: K1, (m1, k5) to end (25 sts).
Beg with a purl row, stocking-st 9 rows.
Dec row: (K2tog, k3) to end (20 sts).
Next and foll 2 alt rows: Purl.
Dec row: (K2tog, k2) to end (15 sts).
Dec row: (K2tog, k1) to end (10 sts).
Dec row: (K2tog) to end (5 sts).
Thread yarn through sts on needle, pull tight and secure.

Making up

Join row ends of Egg leaving a gap. Stuff and close gap.

Roosters are best known for their early morning crowing. During the day, the rooster sits on a high perch looking out for his hens, ready to sound an alarm call if predators approach. However, it is a mistaken belief that hens lay better when there is a rooster around. If a rooster is not present, a hen will often take on the role, stop laying, and begin to crow. There is always a 'boss' chicken in a flock... usually not the rooster.

ROOSTER

DID YOU KNOW?
Chickens lay eggs with or without the help of a rooster.

Information you'll need

Finished size
Rooster measures 6in (15cm) in height

Materials
Any DK yarn:
50g fawn (A)
20g yellow (B)
20g red (C)
20g green (D)
20g orange (E)
20g dark green (F)
20g petrol blue (G)
Oddment of black for features
Note: amounts are generous
but approximate
A pair of 3.25mm (US3:UK10) needles
Acrylic toy stuffing
Knitters' blunt-ended pins and a knitters'
needle for sewing up
Tweezers for stuffing small parts (optional)

Tension
26 sts x 34 rows measure 4in (10cm)
square over stocking-st using 3.25mm
needles and DK yarn before stuffing

Abbreviations
See page 123

How to make Rooster

Body and head

Beg at lower edge using the thumb method and A, cast on 24 sts.

First and foll 10 alt rows (WS): Purl.

Inc row: *(K1, m1) twice, k8, (m1, k1) twice; rep from * once (32 sts).

Inc row: (K1, m1, k14, m1, k1) twice (36 sts).

Inc row: (K1, m1, k16, m1, k1) twice (40 sts).

Inc row: (K1, m1, k18, m1, k1) twice (44 sts).

Inc row: (K1, m1, k20, m1, k1) twice (48 sts).

Inc row: (K1, m1, k22, m1, k1) twice (52 sts).

Inc row: (K1, m1, k24, m1, k1) twice (56 sts).

Inc row: (K1, m1, k26, m1, k1) twice (60 sts).

Inc row: (K1, m1, k28, m1, k1) twice (64 sts).

Inc row: (K1, m1, k30, m1, k1) twice (68 sts).

Inc row: (K1, m1, k32, m1, k1) twice (72 sts).

Next row: Purl.

Inc row: K1, m1, k to last st, m1, k1. Rep last 2 rows once (76 sts).

Beg with a purl row, stocking-st 3 rows.

Inc row: K1, m1, k to last st, m1, k1 (78 sts).

Beg with a purl row, stocking-st 3 rows.

Shape neck

Row 1: K36, turn.

Row 2: S1p, p to end.

Row 3: K33, turn.

Row 4: S1p, p to end.

Row 5: K30, turn.

Row 6: S1p, p to end.

Shape tail

Row 1: K10, turn.

Row 2: S1p, p to end.

Row 3: K2tog, k6, turn (77 sts).

Row 4: S1p, p to end.

Row 5: K2tog, k3, turn (76 sts).

Row 6: S1p, p to end.

Cast off 21 sts at beg of next row (55 sts).

Shape second half of neck

Row 1: P36, turn.

Row 2: S1k, k to end.

Row 3: P33, turn.

Row 4: S1k, k to end.

Row 5: P30, turn.

Row 6: S1k, k to end.

Shape second half of tail

Row 1: P10, turn.

Row 2: S1k, k to end.

Row 3: P2tog, p6, turn (54 sts).

Row 4: S1k, k to end.

Row 5: P2tog, p3, turn (53 sts).

Row 6: S1k, k to end.

Cast off 21 sts p-wise at beg of next row (32 sts).

Stocking-st 12 rows.

Shape top of head

Dec row: (K2, k2tog) to end (24 sts).

Next and foll alt row: Purl.

Dec row: (K1, k2tog) to end (16 sts).

Dec row: (K2tog) to end (8 sts).

Thread yarn through sts on needle, pull tight and secure.

Feet (make 4 pieces)

Using the thumb method and B, cast on 8 sts.

Purl 1 row.

Inc row (RS): K1, (m1, k2) to last st, m1, k1 (12 sts).

Beg with a purl row, stocking-st 3 rows.

****Shape toes**

Next row: K4, turn and work on these 4 sts.

Beg with a purl row, stocking-st 3 rows.

Dec row: K1, k2tog, k1 (3 sts).

Thread yarn through rem sts, pull tight and secure.**

With RS facing, rejoin yarn to sts on needle and rep from ** to ** twice.

Comb (make 2 pieces)

Begin at lower edge using the thumb method and C, cast on 12 sts.

Purl 1 row.

Inc row (RS): K1, (m1, k2) to last st, m1, k1 (18 sts).

****Shape comb**

Next row: P6, turn and work on these 6 sts.

Beg with a knit row, stocking-st 2 rows.

Dec row: K2tog, k2, k2tog (4 sts).

Thread yarn through rem sts, pull tight and secure.**

With WS facing, rejoin yarn to sts on needle and rep from ** to ** twice.

Beak

Using the thumb method and B, cast on 8 sts.

Beg with a purl row, stocking-st 2 rows, ending on a k row.

Dec row: (P2tog) to end (4 sts).

Thread yarn through sts on needle, pull tight and secure.

Crop (make 2)

Begin at top edge using the thumb method and C, cast on 3 sts.

First and foll alt row: Purl.

Inc row: K1, m1, k1, m1, k1 (5 sts).

Inc row: K2, m1, k1, m1, k2 (7 sts).

Beg with a purl row, stocking-st 3 rows.

Dec row: K1, k2tog, k1, k2tog, k1 (5 sts).

Thread yarn through sts on needle, pull tight and secure.

Eye pieces (make 2)

Using the thumb method and C, cast on 6 sts.

First and foll 2 alt rows (WS): Purl.

Inc row: K1, m1, k4, m1, k1 (8 sts).

Shape next row: K1, m1, (k2tog) 3 times, m1, k1 (7 sts).

Dec row: K2tog, k3, k2tog (5 sts).

Dec row: P1, p3tog, p1 (3 sts).

Thread yarn through sts on needle, pull tight and secure.

Wings (make 2)

Using the thumb method and D, cast on 12 sts.

First and foll 2 alt rows (WS): Purl.

Inc row: *(K1, m1) twice, k2, (m1, k1) twice; rep from * once (20 sts).

Inc row: (K1, m1, k8, m1, k1) twice (24 sts).

Inc row: (K1, m1, k10, m1, k1) twice (28 sts).

Beg with a purl row, stocking-st 13 rows.

Dec row: (K2tog, k10, k2tog) twice (24 sts).

Next and foll 3 alt rows: Purl.

Dec row: (K2tog, k8, k2tog) twice (20 sts).

Dec row: (K2tog, k6, k2tog) twice (16 sts).

Dec row: (K2tog, k4, k2tog) twice (12 sts).

Dec row: (K2tog) to end (6 sts).

Thread yarn through sts on needle, pull tight and secure.

Wing patches (make 2)

Using the thumb method and E, cast on 5 sts.

Purl 1 row.

Inc row (RS): K1, (m1, k1) to end (9 sts).

Next row: Purl.

Inc row: K1, m1, k to last st, m1, k1.

Rep last 2 rows once (13 sts).

Beg with a purl row, stocking-st 7 rows.

Dec row: K2tog, k to last 2 sts, k2tog tbl.

Next row: Purl.

Rep last 2 rows twice (7 sts).

Dec row: K2tog, k3tog, k2tog tbl (3 sts).

Thread yarn through sts on needle, pull tight and secure.

Tail feathers

Make 9 in F as foll:

Using the one-needle method and F, cast on 30 sts.

Dec row: K5, (k2tog, k3) 4 times, k5 (26 sts).

Cast off k-wise.

Make 6 in G as foll:

Using the thumb method and G, cast on 25 sts.

Dec row: K8, (k2tog, k3) 3 times, k2 (22 sts).

Cast off k-wise.

Making up

Body and head

Join row ends of head and body and join cast-off stitches at back. Stuff body, pushing stuffing into head and tail. Fold cast-on stitches in half and oversew.

Feet

Place 2 pieces of feet together matching all edges and oversew on right side around toes. Stuff toes, pushing stuffing into toes with tweezers or tip of scissors. Stuff feet and join cast-on stitches. Place Rooster on a flat surface and pin feet to body. Sew in place.

Comb

Place 2 pieces of comb together matching all edges and oversew on right side around shaped row ends. Stuff comb, pushing stuffing in with tweezers or tip of scissors. Join cast-on stitches and pin and sew comb to top of head all the way round lower edge.

Beak

Join row ends of beak and stuff with a tiny ball of stuffing, pushing stuffing in with tweezers or tip of scissors. Sew beak to head all the way round.

Crop

Join row ends of lower half of each piece of crop and stuff lower half with a tiny ball of stuffing, pushing stuffing in with tweezers or tip of scissors. Finish joining row ends of both pieces, place them side by side and sew together. Sew crop to rooster below beak at centre front.

Eye pieces

Sew eye pieces to head using backstitch around outside edge.

rooster

Wings

Fold cast-on stitches of wings in half and oversew. Join row ends of wings on right side and pin and sew to sides of Rooster, all the way round outer edge.

Wing patches

Pin wing patches to wings and sew in place all the way round outer edge.

Tail feathers

Sew tail feathers in F to tip of tail and also to each other at base, 3 in the middle and 6 around this. Sew 6 tail feathers in G above them in the same way.

Features

To make eyes, tie 2 knots in 2 lengths of black yarn, winding the yarn round 6 times to make each knot (see page 120). Tie the eyes to eye pieces and run ends into head.

The collective name for a group of flying ducks is a 'team'; on water they are called a 'paddling'. Ducks are champion swimmers. Even in icy water their feet never get cold as they have no nerves or blood vessels in them. They are also great in the air; some ducks can fly about 332 miles (534km) a day. Mallard ducks launch themselves almost vertically out of the water, reaching a height of about 30ft (9m) before flying horizontally.

DUCK AND DUCKLINGS

DID YOU KNOW?
Very few ducks actually quack. Instead, their calls include squeaks, grunts, groans, chirps, whistles, brays and growls.

DID YOU KNOW?
Ducks have three eyelids on each eye.

Information you'll need

Finished sizes
Duck measures 6½in (16.5cm) in height
Ducklings measure 2in (5cm) in height

Materials
Any DK yarn:
40g white (A)
20g orange (B)
30g yellow (C)
Oddment of black for features
Note: amounts are generous
but approximate
A pair of 3.25mm (US3:UK10) needles
Acrylic toy stuffing
Knitters' blunt-ended pins and a knitters'
needle for sewing up
Tweezers for stuffing small parts (optional)

Tension
26 sts x 34 rows measure 4in (10cm)
square over stocking-st using 3.25mm
needles and DK yarn before stuffing

Abbreviations
See page 123

duck and ducklings

How to make Duck

Body and head

Begin at lower edge using the thumb method and A, cast on 24 sts.

First and foll 8 alt rows (WS): Purl.

Inc row: *(K1, m1) twice, k8, (m1, k1) twice; rep from * once (32 sts).

Inc row: (K1, m1, k14, m1, k1) twice (36 sts).

Inc row: (K1, m1, k16, m1, k1) twice (40 sts).

Inc row: (K1, m1, k18, m1, k1) twice (44 sts).

Inc row: (K1, m1, k20, m1, k1) twice (48 sts).

Inc row: (K1, m1, k22, m1, k1) twice (52 sts).

Inc row: (K1, m1, k24, m1, k1) twice (56 sts).

Inc row: (K1, m1, k26, m1, k1) twice (60 sts).

Inc row: (K1, m1, k28, m1, k1) twice (64 sts).

Next row: Purl.

Inc row: K1, m1, k to last st, m1, k1. Rep last 2 rows once (68 sts).

Beg with a purl row, stocking-st 3 rows.

Inc row: K1, m1, k to last st, m1, k1 (70 sts).

Beg with a purl row, stocking-st 3 rows.

Shape neck

Row 1: K30, turn.

Row 2: S1p, p to end.

Row 3: K24, turn.

Row 4: S1p, p to end.

Shape tail

Row 1: K10, turn.

Row 2: S1p, p to end.

Row 3: K2tog, k6, turn (69 sts).

Row 4: S1p, p to end.

Row 5: K2tog, k3, turn (68 sts).

Row 6: S1p, p to end.

Cast off 18 sts at beg of next row (50 sts).

Shape second half of neck

Row 1: P30, turn.

Row 2: S1k, k to end.

Row 3: P24, turn.

Row 4: S1k, k to end.

Shape second half of tail

Row 1: P10, turn.

Row 2: S1k, k to end.

Row 3: P2tog, p6, turn (49 sts).

Row 4: S1k, k to end.

Row 5: P2tog, p3, turn (48 sts).

Row 6: S1k, k to end.

Cast off 18 sts p-wise at beg of next row (30 sts).

Stocking-st 4 rows.

Dec row: K2tog, k to last 2 sts, k2tog (28 sts).

Beg with a purl row, stocking-st 21 rows.

Shape top of head

Dec row: (K2, k2tog) to end (21 sts).

Next and foll alt row: Purl.

Dec row: (K1, k2tog) to end (14 sts).

Dec row: (K2tog) to end (7 sts).

Thread yarn through sts on needle, pull tight and secure.

Feet (make 4 pieces)

Begin at toes using the thumb method and B, cast on 20 sts.

Purl 1 row.

Dec row (RS): K7, (k3tog) twice, k7 (16 sts).

Shape toes

Row 1: P10, turn.

Row 2: S1k, k3, turn.

Row 3: S1p, p to end.

Dec row: (K2tog, k4, k2tog) twice (12 sts).

Purl 1 row.

Dec row: K2tog, k to last 2 sts, k2tog.

Next row: Purl.

Rep last 2 rows once (8 sts).

Cast off.

Beak

Using the thumb method and B, cast on 16 sts.

Purl 1 row.

Dec row (RS): K5, (k3tog) twice, k5 (12 sts).

Beg with a purl row, stocking-st 5 rows.

Dec row: (K2, k2tog, k2) twice (10 sts).

Purl 1 row.

Dec row: (K2tog) to end (5 sts).

Thread yarn through sts on needle, pull tight and secure.

Wings (make 2)

Using the thumb method and A, cast on 12 sts.

First and foll alt row (WS): Purl.

Inc row: *(K1, m1) twice, k2, (m1, k1) twice; rep from * once (20 sts).

Inc row: (K1, m1, k8, m1, k1) twice (24 sts).

Beg with a purl row, stocking-st 9 rows.

Dec row: (K2tog, k8, k2tog) twice (20 sts).

Beg with a purl row, stocking-st 3 rows.

Dec row: (K2tog, k6, k2tog) twice (16 sts).

Next and foll alt row: Purl.

Dec row: (K2tog, k4, k2tog) twice (12 sts).

Dec row: (K2tog) to end (6 sts).

Thread yarn through sts on needle, pull tight and secure.

Making up
Body and head
Join row ends of head and body and join cast-off stitches at back. Stuff body, pushing stuffing into head, neck and tail. Fold cast-on stitches in half and oversew.

Feet
Place 2 pieces of feet together matching all edges and oversew on right side around toes. Join row ends and stuff, pushing stuffing into toes with tweezers or tip of scissors. Join cast-off stitches, place Duck on a flat surface and pin feet to body. Sew in place.

Beak
Join row ends of beak and stuff. With seam underneath, sew beak to head all the way round.

Wings
Fold cast-on stitches of wings in half and oversew. Join row ends of wings and pin and sew to sides of Duck all the way round outer edge.

Features
To make eyes, tie 2 knots in 2 lengths of black yarn, winding the yarn round 6 times to make each knot (see page 120). Tie eyes to head and run ends into head.

How to make Ducklings
Body and head
Beg at lower edge using the thumb method and C, cast on 6 sts and work in garter-st.
Inc row (RS): (Inc 1) to end (12 sts).
Next and foll alt row: Knit.
Inc row: (K1, inc 1) to end (18 sts).
Inc row: (K2, inc 1) to end (24 sts).
Garter-st 5 rows.
Dec row: K2tog, k to last 2 sts, k2tog.
Next row: Knit.
Rep last 2 rows once (20 sts).
Dec row: (K2tog) twice, k to last 4 sts, (k2tog) twice.
Rep last dec row once (12 sts).
Garter-st 8 rows.
Shape top of head
Dec row: (K2tog) to end (6 sts).
Thread yarn though sts on needle, pull tight and secure.

Wings (make 2)
Beg at lower edge using the thumb method and C, cast on 4 sts and work in garter-st.
Inc row (RS): Inc 1, k2, inc 1 (6 sts).
Next row: Knit.
Dec row: Knit next row and at the same time k2tog at beg for left wing and k2tog tbl at end for right wing.
Rep last 2 rows once (4 sts).
Garter-st 2 rows.
Cast off in garter-st.

Feet (make 2)
Using the thumb method and B, cast on 7 sts.
Cast off p-wise.

Beak
Using the thumb method and B, cast on 5 sts.
Cast off p-wise.

Making up
Body and head
Join row ends of head and body and stuff and join lower edge.

Wings
Place wings either side of Duckling and sew across top edge of each wing to body.

Feet
Fold feet in half. Place Duckling on flat surface and sew feet to Duckling across fold.

Beak
Fold beak and sew open beak to head.

Features
To make eyes, tie 2 knots in 2 lengths of black yarn, winding the yarn round 3 times to make each knot (see page 120). Tie eyes to head and run ends into head.

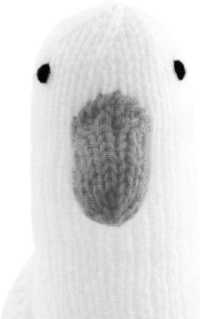

Horses can communicate how they are feeling by their facial expressions. They use their ears, nostrils and eyes to show their moods, such as their dislike for pigs. When they sleep, horses lock the muscles in their legs so they can remain standing and not fall over. Horses expend more energy lying down than they do when standing. They also sleep longer in the summer than in the winter.

HORSE

DID YOU KNOW?
Horses cannot breathe through their mouths.

Information you'll need

Finished size
Horse measures 10in (25cm) in height

Materials
Any DK yarn:
80g brown (A)
10g cream (B)
20g dark brown (C)
40g light brown (D)
Oddments of black and dusky pink
for features
Note: amounts are generous but
approximate
A pair of 3.25mm (US3:UK10) needles
Acrylic toy stuffing
Knitters' blunt-ended pins and a knitters'
needle for sewing up

Tension
26 sts x 34 rows measure 4in (10cm)
square over stocking-st using 3.25mm
needles and DK yarn before stuffing

Abbreviations
See page 123
Special abbreviation: Loop-st
Insert RH needle into next st, place first
finger of LH behind LH needle and wind
yarn clockwise round needle and finger
3 times, then just round needle once.
Knit this st, pulling 4 loops through.
Place loops just made onto LH needle
and knit into the back of them. Pull
loops just made sharply down to secure.
Continue to next st.

DID YOU KNOW?
Most horses live for about
25 years. However, the
oldest horse recorded was
called Old Billy – an English
barge horse that lived to the
grand old age of 62!

How to make Horse

Body back

Beg at lower edge using the thumb method and A, cast on 35 sts.

First and foll 4 alt rows (WS): Purl.

Inc row: K10, m1, k15, m1, k10 (37 sts).

Inc row: K11, m1, k15, m1, k11 (39 sts).

Inc row: K12, m1, k15, m1, k12 (41 sts).

Inc row: K13, m1, k15, m1, k13 (43 sts).

Inc row: K14, m1, k15, m1, k14 (45 sts).

Work hole to attach tail

Next row: P22, yrn, p2tog, p to end.

Stocking-st 10 rows.

Shape sides

Dec row: K2tog, k to last 2 sts, k2tog tbl.

Next row: Purl.

Rep last 2 rows 12 times more (19 sts).

Cast off.

Body front

Work as for body back omitting hole for tail (purl this row).

Base

Using the thumb method and A, cast on 20 sts.

First row (WS): Purl.

Inc row: K1, m1, k to last st, m1, k1.

Rep first 2 rows 5 times more (32 sts).

Beg with a purl row, stocking-st 5 rows.

Dec row: K2tog, k to last 2 sts, k2tog tbl.

Next row: Purl.

Rep last 2 rows 5 times more (20 sts).

Cast off.

Head

Beg at centre back of head using the thumb method and A, cast on 9 sts.

First and foll 5 alt rows (WS): Purl.

Inc row: K1, (m1, k1) to end (17 sts).

Inc row: K1, (m1, k2) to end (25 sts).

Inc row: K1, (m1, k3) to end (33 sts).

Inc row: K1, (m1, k4) to end (41 sts).

Inc row: K1, (m1, k5) to end (49 sts).

Inc row: K1, (m1, k6) to end (57 sts).

Beg with a purl row, stocking-st 13 rows.

Dec row: K11, (k2tog, k1) 12 times, k10 (45 sts).

Beg with a purl row, stocking-st 5 rows.

Dec row: K8, (k2tog, k1) 10 times, k7 (35 sts).

Purl 1 row.

Change to B for muzzle.

Next row: (K1 tbl) to end.

Beg with a purl row, stocking-st 9 rows.

Dec row: K5, (k2tog) 4 times, k9, (k2tog) 4 times, k5 (27 sts).

Purl 1 row.

Dec row: K5, (k2tog) twice, k9, (k2tog) twice, k5 (23 sts).

Cast off p-wise.

Head patch

Using the thumb method and B, cast on 6 sts.

Beg with a purl row, stocking-st 7 rows.

Dec row: K2tog, k2, k2tog tbl (4 sts).

Purl 1 row.

Thread yarn through sts on needle, pull tight and secure.

Hind legs (make 2)

Beg at hoof using the thumb method and C, cast on 8 sts.

First row (WS): Purl.

Inc row: K1, (m1, k1) to end (15 sts).

Rep first 2 rows once (29 sts).

Beg with a purl row, stocking-st 11 rows.

Change to A and dec.

Dec row: K6, (k2tog, k1) 6 times, k5 (23 sts).

Beg with a purl row, stocking-st 15 rows.

Cast off.

Forelegs (make 2)

Beg at hoof using the thumb method and C, cast on 7 sts.

First row (WS): Purl.

Inc row: K1, (m1, k1) to end.

Rep first 2 rows once (25 sts).

Beg with a purl row, stocking-st 9 rows.

Change to A and dec.

Dec row: (K3, k2tog) to end (20 sts).

Beg with a purl row, stocking-st 21 rows.

Dec row: (K2, k2tog) to end (15 sts).

Purl 1 row.

Dec row: (K1, k2tog) to end (10 sts).

Thread yarn through sts on needle, pull tight and secure.

Ears (make 2)

Beg at lower edge using the thumb method and A, cast on 16 sts.

Beg with a purl row, stocking-st 5 rows.

Dec row: *K2, (k2tog) twice, k2; rep from * once (12 sts).

Purl 1 row.

Dec row: (K2tog) to end (6 sts).

Thread yarn through sts on needle, pull tight and secure.

Fringe

Using the thumb method and D, cast on 8 sts loosely.

First row: K1, (loop-st) to last st, k1.

Next row: K2tog, k to last 2 sts, k2tog tbl (6 sts).

Rep loop-st row once.

Cast off k-wise, then cut all loops.

Mane

Using the thumb method and D, cast on 4 sts loosely.

First row: K1, (loop-st) twice, k1.

Next row: Knit.

Rep first 2 rows 10 times more, then loop-st row once.

Cast off k-wise, then cut all loops.

Making up

Tail
Make a 4in (10cm) tassel out of D with approximately 60 strands in tassel (see page 121). Using A, gather round hole in back of Horse. Insert folded end of tail and sew in place securely.

Body
Place the two halves of the body together matching all edges and join row ends. Stuff body leaving neck and lower edge open, filling out base with plenty of stuffing.

Base
Pin base to lower edge of body and sew base to body leaving a gap. Adjust stuffing in base, adding more stuffing if needed, and close gap.

Head
Join row ends of muzzle and with this seam at centre of underneath side, join cast-off stitches. Gather round cast-on stitches, pull tight and secure. Join row ends of head leaving a gap, stuff, pushing stuffing into muzzle and top of head, and close gap. Pin and sew head to body, adding more stuffing to body if needed.

Hind legs
Gather round cast-on stitches of hind legs, pull tight and secure. Join row ends of hind legs and stuff, pushing a ball of stuffing into hoof. Place body on a flat surface and pin hind legs to body. Sew cast-off stitches of hind legs to body all the way round.

Forelegs
Gather round cast-on stitches of forelegs, pull tight and secure. Join row ends leaving a gap, stuff, pushing a ball of stuffing into hoof, and close gap. Sew forelegs to each side of body, sewing stitches pulled tight on a thread to neck.

Head patch
Place head patch at centre front of head and sew all edges down.

Ears
Join row ends of ears on right side and with this seam at centre of inside edge, join lower edge. Fold ears slightly and sew to head.

Fringe and mane
Place fringe between ears and sew down all edges. Sew mane from top of head down back of head, sewing down all edges.

Features
To make eyes, tie 2 knots in 2 lengths of black yarn, winding the yarn round 6 times to make each knot (see page 120). Tie eyes to head and run ends into head. Work nostrils in the same way using dusky pink, winding the yarn round 6 times to make each knot, and tie to muzzle, running ends into muzzle.

DID YOU KNOW?
Little Pumpkin was the smallest horse in history, standing at just 14in (35cm).

Cats are one of the sleepiest mammals. Each day they sleep for around 16 hours; therefore, a seven-year-old cat has only been awake for two years of its life! Despite cat napping so often, a female cat can still have more than 100 kittens in her lifetime. Her kittens begin dreaming at just over one week old. The colour of their eyes changes as they grow older.

CAT

DID YOU KNOW?
A cat's heart beats twice as fast as a human heart.

Information you'll need

Finished size
Cat measures 8in (20cm) in height

Materials
Any DK yarn:
40g grey (A)
20g white (B)
Oddment of black for features
Note: amounts are generous
but approximate
A pair of 3.25mm (US3:UK10) needles
Acrylic toy stuffing
Knitters' blunt-ended pins and a knitters'
needle for sewing up

Tension
26 sts x 34 rows measure 4in (10cm)
square over stocking-st using 3.25mm
needles and DK yarn before stuffing

Abbreviations
See page 123

cat

How to make Cat

Body (make 2 pieces)

Beg at lower edge using the thumb method and A, cast on 30 sts.

First and foll 2 alt rows (WS): Purl.

Inc row: K9, m1, k12, m1, k9 (32 sts).

Inc row: K10, m1, k12, m1, k10 (34 sts).

Inc row: K11, m1, k12, m1, k11 (36 sts).

Beg with a purl row, stocking-st 11 rows.

Shape sides

Dec row: K2tog, k to last 2 sts, k2tog tbl.

Beg with a purl row, stocking-st 3 rows.

Rep last 4 rows twice (30 sts).

Dec row: K2tog, k to last 2 sts, k2tog tbl.

Next row: Purl.

Rep last 2 rows 6 times more (16 sts).

Cast off.

Base

Using thumb method and A, cast on 14 sts.

First row (WS): Purl.

Inc row: K1, m1, k to last st, m1, k1.

Rep first 2 rows 4 times more (24 sts).

Beg with a purl row, stocking-st 5 rows.

Dec row: K2tog, k to last 2 sts, k2tog tbl.

Next row: Purl.

Rep last 2 rows 4 times more (14 sts).

Cast off.

Head

Beg at centre back of head using the thumb method and A, cast on 9 sts.

First and foll 5 alt rows (WS): Purl.

Inc row: K1, (m1, k1) to end (17 sts).

Inc row: K1, (m1, k2) to end (25 sts).

Inc row: K1, (m1, k3) to end (33 sts).

Inc row: K1, (m1, k4) to end (41 sts).

Inc row: K1, (m1, k5) to end (49 sts).

Inc row: K1, (m1, k6) to end (57 sts).

Beg with a purl row, stocking-st 5 rows.

Join on B and work in stripes, carrying yarn loosely up side of work.

Stocking-st 2 rows B, then stocking-st 4 rows A.

Dec row: Using B, k8, (k2tog, k1) 14 times, k7 (43 sts).

Purl 1 row B, then stocking-st 2 rows A.

Dec row: Using A, k4, (k2tog, k1) 12 times, k3 (31 sts).

Purl 1 row A. Cont in B only.

Next row: (K1 tbl) to end.

Next row: Purl.

Dec row: K2tog, k to last 2 sts, k2tog tbl.

Rep last 2 rows once (27 sts).

Next row: Purl.

Dec row: K3, (k2tog) 4 times, k5, (k2tog) 4 times, k3 (19 sts).

Purl 1 row.

Dec row: K1, (k2tog) 4 times, k1, (k2tog) 4 times, k1 (11 sts).

Dec row: P1, (p2tog) twice, p1, (p2tog) twice, p1 (7 sts).

Thread yarn through sts on needle, pull tight and secure.

Hind legs (make 2)

Beg at paw using the thumb method and B, cast on 7 sts.

First row (WS): Purl.

Inc row: K1, (m1, k1) to end.

Rep first 2 rows once (25 sts).

Beg with a purl row, stocking-st 7 rows.

Dec row: K4, (k2tog, k1) 6 times, k3 (19 sts).

Beg with a purl row, stocking-st 3 rows.

Join on A and work in stripes, carrying yarn loosely up side of work.

Stocking-st 2 rows A, 4 rows B, 2 rows A, then 4 rows B.

Cast off in B.

Forelegs (make 2)

Beg at paw using the thumb method and B, cast on 6 sts.

First row (WS): Purl.

Inc row: K1, (m1, k1) to end.

Rep first 2 rows once (21 sts).

Beg with a purl row, stocking-st 7 rows.

Join on B and work in stripes, carrying yarn loosely up side of work and dec.

Dec row: Using A, k2, (k2tog, k1) 6 times, k1 (15 sts).

Using A, purl 1 row.

Stocking-st 4 rows B, then 2 rows A and rep these 6 striped rows once.

Cont in B only and stocking-st 2 rows.

Dec row: (K1, k2tog) to end (10 sts).

Purl 1 row.

Thread yarn though sts on needle, pull tight and secure.

Ears (make 2)

Beg at lower edge using the thumb method and A, cast on 16 sts.

Beg with a purl row, stocking-st 3 rows.

Dec row (RS): *K2, (k2tog) twice, k2; rep from * once (12 sts).

Next and foll alt row: Purl.

Dec row: *K1, (k2tog) twice, k1; rep from * once (8 sts).

Dec row: (K2tog) to end (4 sts).

Thread yarn through sts on needle, pull tight and secure.

Tail

Beg at base of tail using the thumb method and A, cast on 24 sts.

Beg with a purl row, stocking-st 9 rows.

Join in B and work in stripes, carrying yarn loosely up side of work and dec.

Dec row: Using B, k2tog, k to end.

Using B, purl 1 row.

Stocking-st 4 rows A.

Rep last 6 rows 6 times more (17 sts).

Cont in A only and dec.

Dec row: K2tog, k to end (16 sts).

Beg with a purl row, stocking-st 7 rows.

Dec row: (K2tog) to end (8 sts).

Thread yarn through sts on needle and leave loose.

Making up

Body
Place the two halves of the body together matching all edges and join row ends. Stuff body leaving neck and lower edge open, filling out base with plenty of stuffing.

Base
Pin base to lower edge of body and sew base to body leaving a gap. Adjust stuffing in base, adding more stuffing to body if needed, and close gap.

Head
Gather round cast-on stitches, pull tight and secure. Join row ends of head leaving a gap, stuff, pushing stuffing into nose and top of head, and close gap. Pin and sew head to body, adding more stuffing to body if needed.

Hind legs
Gather round cast-on stitches of hind legs, pull tight and secure. Join row ends of hind legs and stuff. Place body on a flat surface and pin and sew cast-off stitches of hind legs to body all the way round.

Forelegs
Gather round cast-on stitches of forelegs, pull tight and secure. Join row ends of forelegs leaving a gap, stuff and close gap. Sew forelegs to body at shoulders.

Ears
Join row ends of ears and with this seam at centre back, sew ears to head behind white stripe at top of head.

Tail
Roll tail up, starting at base of edge with shaped row ends, towards straight row ends, pull stitches tight on a thread and secure. Catch straight row ends in place and sew tail to back of Cat.

Features
To make eyes, tie 2 knots in 2 lengths of black yarn, winding the yarn round 6 times to make each knot (see page 120). Tie knots to head on stripe in A with 5 clear knitted stitches in between and run ends into head. Embroider nose, working 3 horizontal stitches close together over 2 stitches for nose. Embroider mouth and whiskers using straight stitches as shown in picture. (See page 120 for how to begin and fasten off invisibly for embroidery.)

cat

DID YOU KNOW?
Sir Isaac Newton, discoverer of the principles of gravity, also invented the cat flap.

Herding dogs, often referred to as sheepdogs, are a common sight on farms. They respond to a variety of herding commands, indicated by a hand movement, whistle or voice. Different breeds herd animals in different ways. Some breeds, such as the Australian Cattle Dog, nip the heels of animals to control them, while the Border Collie, for instance, gets in front of the animals and stares them into submission!

SHEEPDOG

Information you'll need

Finished size
Sheepdog measures 8in (20cm) in height

Materials
Any DK yarn:
40g black (A)
30g white (B)
Note: amounts are generous
but approximate
A pair of 3.25mm (US3:UK10) needles
Acrylic toy stuffing
Knitters' blunt-ended pins and a knitters'
needle for sewing up

Tension
26 sts x 34 rows measure 4in (10cm)
square over stocking-st using 3.25mm
needles and DK yarn before stuffing

Abbreviations
See page 123

DID YOU KNOW?
The Basenji dog is the only
dog that is not able to bark.

sheepdog

How to make Sheepdog

Body (make 2 pieces)

Beg at lower edge using the thumb method and A, cast on 30 sts.

First and foll 2 alt rows (WS): Purl.

Inc row: K9, m1, k12, m1, k9 (32 sts).

Inc row: K10, m1, k12, m1, k10 (34 sts).

Inc row: K11, m1, k12, m1, k11 (36 sts).

Beg with a purl row, stocking-st 11 rows.

Shape sides

Dec row: K2tog, k to last 2 sts, k2tog tbl.

Beg with a purl row, stocking-st 3 rows.

Rep last 4 rows twice (30 sts).

Dec row: K2tog, k to last 2 sts, k2tog tbl.

Next row: Purl.

Rep last 2 rows 6 times more (16 sts).

Cast off.

Base

Using the thumb method and A, cast on 14 sts.

First row (WS): Purl.

Inc row: K1, m1, k to last st, m1, k1.

Rep first 2 rows 4 times more (24 sts).

Beg with a purl row, stocking-st 5 rows.

Dec row: K2tog, k to last 2 sts, k2tog tbl.

Next row: Purl.

Rep last 2 rows 4 times more (14 sts).

Cast off.

Head

Beg at centre back of head using the thumb method and B, cast on 10 sts.

First and foll 4 alt rows (WS): Purl.

Inc row: K1, (m1, k1) to end (19 sts).

Inc row: K1, (m1, k2) to end (28 sts).

Inc row: K1, (m1, k3) to end (37 sts).

Inc row: K1, (m1, k4) to end (46 sts).

Inc row: K1, (m1, k5) to end (55 sts).

Beg with a purl row, stocking-st 13 rows.

Dec row: K10, (k2tog, k1) 12 times, k9 (43 sts).

Beg with a purl row, stocking-st 3 rows.

Dec row: K7, (k2tog, k1) 10 times, k6 (33 sts).

Next and foll alt row: Purl.

Next row: (K1 tbl) to end.

Dec row: K5, (k2tog, k1) 8 times, k4 (25 sts).

Beg with a purl row, stocking-st 5 rows.

Dec row: (K3, k2tog) to end (20 sts).

Purl 1 row.

Dec row: (K2tog) to end (10 sts).

Thread yarn through sts on needle, pull tight and secure.

Hind legs (make 2)

Beg at paw using the thumb method and B, cast on 8 sts.

First row (WS): Purl.

Inc row: K1, (m1, k1) to end.

Rep first 2 rows once (29 sts).

Beg with a purl row, stocking-st 9 rows.

Dec row: K3, (k2tog, k1) 8 times, k2 (21 sts).

Purl 1 row.

Change to A and stocking-st 12 rows.

Cast off.

Forelegs (make 2)

Beg at paw using the thumb method and B, cast on 7 sts.

First row (WS): Purl.

Inc row: K1, (m1, k1) to end.

Rep first 2 rows once (25 sts).

Beg with a purl row, stocking-st 5 rows.

Dec row: K4, (k2tog, k1) 6 times, k3 (19 sts).

Purl 1 row.

Change to A and stocking-st 14 rows.

Dec row: K1, (k2tog, k1) to end.

Next row: Purl.

Rep last 2 rows once (9 sts).

Thread yarn through sts on needle, pull tight and secure.

Ears (make 2)

Using the thumb method and A, cast on 4 sts.

Purl 1 row.

Inc row (RS): K1, (m1, k1) to end (7 sts).

Next row: Purl.

Inc row: K1, m1, k to last st, m1, k1.

Rep last 2 rows twice (13 sts).

Beg with a purl row, stocking-st 11 rows.

Dec row: K1, (k2tog, k1) to end (9 sts).

Purl 1 row.

Dec row: (K2tog) twice, k1, (k2tog) twice (5 sts).

Thread yarn through sts on needle, pull tight and secure.

Nose

Using the thumb method and A, cast on 5 sts.

Purl 1 row.

Dec row: K2tog, k1, k2tog tbl (3 sts).

Thread yarn through sts on needle, pull tight and secure.

Tail

Using the thumb method and A, cast on 20 sts.

Beg with purl row, stocking-st 25 rows.

Change to B and stocking-st 4 rows.

Dec row: K2tog, k to end.

Next row: Purl.

Rep last 2 rows 4 times more (15 sts).

Dec row: (K2tog, k1) to end (10 sts).

Thread yarn though sts on needle and leave loose.

DID YOU KNOW?
The oldest dog on record was named Bluey, who lived 29 years and 5 months. In human years he was 203 years old.

DID YOU KNOW?
Each dog can be identified by its unique nose print, much like a human's fingerprint.

Making up

Body

Place the two halves of the body together matching all edges and join row ends. Stuff body leaving neck and lower edge open, filling out base with plenty of stuffing.

Base

Pin base to lower edge of body and sew base to body leaving a gap. Adjust stuffing in base, adding more stuffing if needed, and close gap.

Head

Gather round cast-on stitches of head, pull tight and secure. Join row ends leaving a gap, stuff, pushing stuffing into nose and top of head and close gap. Pin and sew head to body, adding more stuffing to body if needed.

Hind legs

Gather round cast-on stitches of hind legs, pull tight and secure. Join row ends of hind legs and stuff. Place body on a flat surface and pin and sew cast-off stitches of hind legs to body all the way round.

Forelegs

Gather round cast-on stitches of forelegs, pull tight and secure. Join row ends leaving a gap, stuff and close gap. Sew forelegs to each side of body.

Ears

Join row ends of ears by oversewing on right side, and with these seams facing inwards and the ear pointing upwards, sew cast-on stitches and approx ½in (1cm) of shaped row ends of ears to either side of head. Fold ears forwards and catch in place.

Tail

Roll tail up, starting at base of edge with shaped row ends, towards straight row ends, pull stitches tight on a thread and secure. Catch straight row ends in place. To make tail curved, sew a running stitch along inside edge of curve, pull slightly and secure. Sew tail to back of Sheepdog.

Features

To make eyes, tie 2 knots in 2 lengths of black yarn, winding the yarn round 6 times to make each knot (see page 120). Now tie eyes to head with 4 clear stitches in between and run ends into head. Sew nose to centre front of muzzle and embroider mouth using straight stitches in black, as shown in picture. Embroider 3 toes in black on hind legs and forelegs, taking 2 short stitches close together for each toe. (See page 120 for how to begin and fasten off invisibly for the embroidery.)

Goats have been found living in areas as high as 13,000ft (4,000m) – that's almost half the height of Mount Everest. As well as their head for heights, goats are well known for their agility, athletic abilities and intelligence. They are extremely curious creatures and will pick up things with their mouths to investigate them. However, contrary to popular belief, goats have sensitive stomachs and are therefore very picky eaters. They also have sensitive lips and, interestingly, no upper front teeth.

GOAT

DID YOU KNOW?
Both male and female goats can have beards.

Information you'll need

Finished size
Goat measures 8½in (21.5cm) in height

Materials
Any DK yarn:
80g beige (A)
20g biscuit (B)
10g light brown (C)
10g cream (D)
Oddment of black for features
Note: amounts are generous
but approximate
A pair of 3.25mm (US3:UK10) needles
Acrylic toy stuffing
A pipe cleaner
Knitters' blunt-ended pins and a knitters'
needle for sewing up
Tweezers for stuffing small parts (optional)

Tension
26 sts x 34 rows measure 4in (10cm)
square over stocking-st using 3.25mm
needles and DK yarn before stuffing

Abbreviations
See page 123

goat

How to make Goat

Body (make 2 pieces)
Beg at lower edge using the thumb method and A, cast on 32 sts.
First and foll 3 alt rows (WS): Purl.
Inc row: K9, m1, k14, m1, k9 (34 sts).
Inc row: K10, m1, k14, m1, k10 (36 sts).
Inc row: K11, m1, k14, m1, k11 (38 sts).
Inc row: K12, m1, k14, m1, k12 (40 sts).
Beg with a purl row, stocking-st 11 rows.
Shape sides
Dec row: K2tog, k to last 2 sts, k2tog tbl.
Next row: Purl.
Rep last 2 rows 11 times more (16 sts).
Cast off.

Base
Using the thumb method and A, cast on 16 sts.
First row (WS): Purl.
Inc row: K1, m1, k to last st, m1, k1.
Rep first 2 rows 4 times more (26 sts).
Beg with a purl row, stocking-st 5 rows.
Dec row: K2tog, k to last 2 sts, k2tog tbl.
Next row: Purl.
Rep last 2 rows 4 times more (16 sts).
Cast off.

Head
Beg at centre back of head using the thumb method and A, cast on 9 sts.
First and foll 4 alt rows (WS): Purl.
Inc row: K1, (m1, k1) to end (17 sts).
Inc row: K1, (m1, k2) to end (25 sts).
Inc row: K1, (m1, k3) to end (33 sts).
Inc row: K1, (m1, k4) to end (41 sts).
Inc row: K1, (m1, k5) to end (49 sts).
Beg with a purl row, stocking-st 13 rows.
Dec row: K6, (k2tog, k3) 8 times, k3 (41 sts).
Beg with a purl row, stocking-st 3 rows.
Dec row: K7, (k2tog, k3) 6 times, k4 (35 sts).
Beg with a purl row, stocking-st 3 rows.
Dec row: (K3, k2tog) to end (28 sts).

Beg with a purl row, stocking-st 5 rows.
Dec row: (K2, k2tog) to end (21 sts).
Next and foll alt row: Purl.
Dec row: (K1, k2tog) to end (14 sts).
Dec row: (K2tog) to end (7 sts).
Thread yarn through sts on needle, pull tight and secure.

Hind legs (make 2)
Beg at hoof using the thumb method and B, cast on 16 sts.
Purl 1 row.
Inc row (RS): K2, (m1, k2) to end (23 sts).
Beg with a purl row, stocking-st 7 rows.
Change to A and beg with a knit row, stocking-st 2 rows.
Inc row: K1, m1, k to last 2 sts, m1, k1 (25 sts).
Beg with a purl row, stocking-st 11 rows.
Cast off.

Forelegs (make 2)
Beg at hoof using the thumb method and B, cast on 14 sts.
Purl 1 row.
Inc row: K2, (m1, k2) to end (20 sts).
Beg with a purl row, stocking-st 7 rows.
Change to A and beg with a knit row, stocking-st 16 rows.
Dec row: K1, k2tog, (k2, k2tog) to last st, k1 (15 sts).
Cast off p-wise.

Horns (make 2)
Beg at lower edge using the thumb method and C, cast on 8 sts and work in garter-st.
Garter-st 6 rows.
Dec row: K2tog, k to end.
Garter-st 3 rows.
Rep last 4 rows once (6 sts).
Thread yarn through sts on needle, pull tight and secure.

Ears (make 2)
Beg at base edge using the thumb method and A, cast on 10 sts.
Beg with a purl row, stocking-st 5 rows.
Dec row: K2, (k2tog, k2) twice (8 sts).
Purl 1 row.
Dec row: K2, (k2tog) twice, k2 (6 sts).
Thread yarn through sts on needle, pull tight and secure.

Beard
Beg at top edge using the thumb method and D, cast on 10 sts.
Row 1 (WS): P7, turn.
Row 2: S1k, k to end.
Row 3: Purl.
Row 4: K7, turn.
Row 5: S1p, p to end.
Beg with a knit row, stocking-st 2 rows.
Dec row: K2, (k2tog, k2) twice (8 sts).
Purl 1 row.
Dec row: K2, (k2tog) twice, k2 (6 sts).
Thread yarn through sts on needle, pull tight and secure.

Tail
Beg at base using the thumb method and A, cast on 14 sts.
Beg with a purl row, stocking-st 5 rows.
Dec row: K2tog, k to last 2 sts, k2tog tbl.
Next row: Purl.
Rep last 2 rows twice (8 sts).
Dec row: (K2tog) to end (4 sts).
Thread yarn through sts on needle, pull tight and secure.

DID YOU KNOW?
A group of goats is known as a 'trip' or a 'tribe'.

Making up

Body
Place the two halves of body together matching all edges and join row ends. Stuff body leaving neck and lower edge open, filling out base with plenty of stuffing.

Base
Pin base to lower edge of body and sew base to body leaving a gap. Adjust stuffing in base, adding more stuffing if needed, and close gap.

Head
Gather round cast-on stitches of head, pull tight and secure. Join row ends of head leaving a gap, stuff head, pushing stuffing into snout and top of head. Finish joining row ends and pin and sew head to body, adding more stuffing to body if needed.

Hind legs
Join row ends of hooves and with seam at centre of underneath side, join cast-on stitches. Join row ends of hind legs and stuff legs. Place body on a flat surface and pin hind legs to body. Sew cast-off stitches of hind legs to body all the way round.

Forelegs
Fold cast-on stitches of forelegs in half and oversew. Join row ends of forelegs and stuff. With seam at centre of inside edge, oversew cast-off stitches. Sew forelegs to each side of body, sewing cast-on stitches to neck.

Horns
Cut the pipe cleaner in half and fold each piece in half. Join row ends of horns and place each folded end of pipe cleaner into horns. Stuff horns, pushing stuffing in with tweezers or tip of scissors, and trim excess pipe cleaners. Sew horns to head with 7 clear knitted stitches in between and bend horns outwards.

Ears
Join row ends of ears and with this seam at centre front, fold base of each ear in half and catch in place. Sew ears to head at each side below horns.

Beard
Join row ends of beard and lightly stuff beard, pushing stuffing in with tweezers or tip of scissors. With seam at centre back, sew to underneath of chin.

Tail
Join row ends of tail and stuff. Sew cast-on stitches to centre back of Goat.

Features
To make eyes, tie 2 knots in 2 lengths of black yarn, winding the yarn round 6 times to make each knot (see page 120). Tie knots to head with 5 clear knitted stitches in between and run ends into head. Embroider nose and mouth in black, using straight stitches as shown in picture. (See page 120 for how to begin and fasten off invisibly for the embroidery.)

goat

Highland bulls are easily identified by their exceptionally hairy coats and their long, lustrous fringes; however, their most notable feature are their distinctive sweeping horns, which are used to dig through thick snow to find vegetation lying underneath. Although they primarily eat grasses, Highland bulls are also rather partial to the occasional leaf or pretty flower.

HIGHLAND BULL

DID YOU KNOW?
Highland bulls tend to be quiet and charming, demonstrating superior intelligence and patience.

Information you'll need

Finished size
Highland Bull measures 10in (25cm) in height

Materials
Any DK yarn:
80g ginger (A)
40g brown (B)
10g biscuit (C)
Oddment of black for features
Note: amounts are generous but approximate
A pair of 3.25 (US3:UK10) needles
Acrylic toy stuffing
2 pipe cleaners
Knitters' blunt-ended pins and a knitters' needle for sewing up
Tweezers for stuffing small parts (optional)

Tension
26 sts x 34 rows measure 4in (10cm) square over stocking-st using 3.25mm needles and DK yarn before stuffing

Abbreviations
See page 123
Special abbreviation: Loop-st
Insert RH needle into next st, place first finger of LH behind LH needle and wind yarn clockwise round needle and finger 3 times, then just round needle once. Knit this st pulling 4 loops through. Place loops just made onto LH needle and knit into the back of them. Pull loops just made sharply down to secure. Continue to next st.

highland bull

How to make Bull

Body (make 2 pieces)
Beg at lower edge using the thumb method and A, cast on 35 sts.
First and foll 4 alt rows (WS): Purl.
Inc row: K10, m1, k15, m1, k10 (37 sts).
Inc row: K11, m1, k15, m1, k11 (39 sts).
Inc row: K12, m1, k15, m1, k12 (41 sts).
Inc row: K13, m1, k15, m1, k13 (43 sts).
Inc row: K14, m1, k15, m1, k14 (45 sts).
Beg with a purl row, stocking-st 11 rows.
Shape sides
Dec row: K2tog, k to last 2 sts, k2tog tbl.
Next row: Purl.
Rep last 2 rows 12 times more (19 sts).
Cast off.

Base
Using the thumb method and A, cast on 20 sts.
First row (WS): Purl.
Inc row: K1, m1, k to last st, m1, k1.
Rep first 2 rows 5 times more (32 sts).
Beg with a purl row, stocking-st 5 rows.
Dec row: K2tog, k to last 2 sts, k2tog tbl.
Next row: Purl.
Rep last 2 rows 5 times more (20 sts).
Cast off.

Head
Beg at centre of underneath using the thumb method and A, cast on 30 sts.
Place a marker at centre of cast-on edge.
First and next foll alt row (WS): Purl.
Inc row: K4, (m1, k2) 4 times, k8, (m1, k2) 4 times, k2 (38 sts).
Inc row: K6, (m1, k2) 4 times, k12, (m1, k2) 4 times, k4 (46 sts).
Beg with a purl row, stocking-st 25 rows.
Dec row: K8, (k2tog) 4 times, k14, (k2tog) 4 times, k8 (38 sts).
Next and foll alt row: Purl.
Dec row: K6, (k2tog) 4 times, k10, (k2tog) 4 times, k6 (30 sts).
Dec row: K4, (k2tog) 4 times, k6, (k2tog) 4 times, k4 (22 sts).
Cast off p-wise.

Muzzle
Using the thumb method and B, cast on 28 sts.
Beg with a purl row, stocking-st 9 rows.
Dec row: K3, (k2tog) 4 times, k6, (k2tog) 4 times, k3 (20 sts).
Purl 1 row.
Dec row: K3, (k2tog) twice, k6, (k2tog) twice, k3 (16 sts).
Purl 1 row.
Cast off.

Hind legs (make 2)
Beg at hoof using the thumb method and B, cast on 18 sts.
Purl 1 row.
Inc row (RS): K2, (m1, k2) to end (26 sts).
Beg with a purl row, stocking-st 9 rows.
Change to A and dec.
Dec row: K2, (k2tog, k2) to end (20 sts).
Beg with a purl row, stocking-st 3 rows.
Inc row: (K2, m1) twice, k12, (m1, k2) twice (24 sts).
Next and foll alt row: Purl.
Inc row: (K2, m1) twice, k16, (m1, k2) twice (28 sts).
Inc row: (K2, m1) twice, k20, (m1, k2) twice (32 sts).
Beg with a purl row, stocking-st 11 rows.
Cast off.

Forelegs (make 2)
Beg at hoof using the thumb method and B, cast on 14 sts.
Purl 1 row.
Inc row: K2, (m1, k2) to end (20 sts).
Beg with a purl row, stocking-st 7 rows.
Change to A and dec.
Dec row: (K2, k2tog) to end (15 sts).
Beg with a purl row, stocking-st 3 rows.
Inc row: K3, (m1, k3) to end (19 sts).
Beg with a purl row, stocking-st 5 rows.
Inc row: K7, m1, k5, m1, k7 (21 sts).
Beg with a purl row, stocking-st 3 rows.
Inc row: K8, m1, k5, m1, k8 (23 sts).
Beg with a purl row, stocking-st 13 rows.
Dec row: K2tog, (k1, k2tog) to end (15 sts).
Purl 1 row.
Thread yarn through sts on needle, pull tight and secure.

Horns (make 2)

Using the thumb method and C, cast on
8 sts.
Beg with a purl row, stocking-st 13 rows.
Dec row: K3, k2tog, k3 (7 sts).
Next and foll 2 alt rows: Purl.
Dec row: K3, k2tog, k2 (6 sts).
Dec row: K2, k2tog, k2 (5 sts).
Dec row: K1, k2tog, k2 (4 sts).
Thread yarn through sts on needle,
pull tight and secure.

Ears (make 2)

Using the thumb method and B, cast on
8 sts.
Purl 1 row.
Inc row: K1, (m1, k2) to last st, m1, k1
(12 sts).
Beg with a purl row, stocking-st 5 rows.
Dec row: (K1, k2tog) to end (8 sts).
Purl 1 row.
Dec row: (K2tog) to end (4 sts).
Thread yarn through sts on needle,
pull tight and secure.

Fringe

Using the thumb method and A, cast on
6 sts loosely.
First row: K1, (loop-st) to last st, k1.
Cast on 3 sts at beg and end of next row
and knit this row (12 sts).
Next row: K1, (loop-st) to last st, k1.
Next row: Knit.
Rep last 2 rows once.
Next row: K3, (loop-st) 6 times, k3.
Cast off.

Making up

Body

Place the two halves of the body together
matching all edges and join row ends. Stuff
body leaving neck and lower edge open,
filling out base with plenty of stuffing.

Base

Pin base to lower edge of body and sew
base to body leaving a gap. Adjust stuffing
in base, adding more stuffing if needed,
and close gap.

Head

Join row ends of head and with this seam
at centre back, join cast-off stitches. Stuff
head and bring seam and marker together
and oversew cast-on stitches. Pin and sew
head to body, adding more stuffing to
body if needed.

Muzzle

Join row ends of muzzle and with this
seam at centre of underneath side, join
cast-off sts. Stuff muzzle and sew cast-on
stitches of muzzle to lower half of head
all the way round.

Hind legs

Join row ends of hooves and with seam
at centre of underneath side, join
cast-on stitches. Join row ends of hind
legs. Place a ball of stuffing into each
hoof and stuff hind legs. Place body
on a flat surface and pin hind legs to
body. Sew cast-off stitches of hind legs
to body all the way round.

Forelegs

Fold cast-on stitches of forelegs in half and
join. Join row ends of forelegs leaving a
gap and place a small ball of stuffing into
each hoof. Stuff forelegs and close gap.
Sew forelegs to body at shoulders.

Horns

Take a pipe cleaner for each horn and fold
each one in half. Place folded end into
stitches pulled tight on a thread on wrong
side and join row ends of horns around
pipe cleaner, pushing in a little stuffing
with tweezers or tip of scissors. Fold in
excess ends of pipe cleaner. Gather round
cast-on stitches of horns, pull tight and
secure. Sew horns to head and curl tips
of horns upwards.

Ears

Join row ends of ears and with the seam at
centre back, fold each ear in half and catch
in place. Sew ears to each side of head.

Fringe

Place fringe on head and sew cast-off
stitches of fringe to seam at top of head.
Sew all other edges of fringe down.

Tail

Make a twisted cord out of 8 strands of A,
each piece 30in (75cm) long (see page 120).
Tie a knot 2½in (6cm) from folded end and
trim ends beyond knot to 1in (2.5cm). Sew
folded end of tail to Highland Bull at back.

Features

To make eyes, tie 2 knots in 2 lengths
of black yarn, winding the yarn round 6
times to make each knot (see page 120).
Tie eyes to head and run ends into head.
Work nostrils in the same way using C and
tie to muzzle, running ends into muzzle.

highland bull

Male sheep are called rams, and their horns serve as an imposing status symbol. A ram's horns are used for dominance and as weapons during battles for mating rights. When rams fight, they do so by facing each other and running at full force. When male mountain bighorn sheep charge, they can reach speeds of 20mph (32km/h)! Battles can continue for hours until one of the rams walks away. Fortunately they have thick skulls, preventing serious injuries from occurring.

RAM

DID YOU KNOW?
Some rams have heavily spiralled horns, some even have four horns, while some breeds have no horns at all.

DID YOU KNOW?

The heaviest sheep was a ram called Stradford Whisper. In March 1991 he weighed 545lb (247kg) and was a little over 3ft (1m) high!

Information you'll need

Measurement
Ram measures 8½in (21.5cm) in height

Materials
Any DK yarn:
80g cream (A)
20g beige (B)
Oddment of dark brown for features
Note: amounts are generous
but approximate
A pair of 3.25mm (US3:UK10) needles
Acrylic toy stuffing
Knitters' blunt-ended pins and a knitters'
needle for sewing up
Tweezers for stuffing small parts (optional)

Tension
26 sts x 34 rows measure 4in (10cm)
square over rev stocking-st using 3.25mm
needles and DK yarn before stuffing

Abbreviations
See page 123

ram

How to make Ram

Body (make 2 pieces)

Beg at lower edge using the thumb method and A, cast on 32 sts and work in rev stocking-st.

First and foll 3 alt rows (RS): Purl.
Inc row: K9, m1, k14, m1, k9 (34 sts).
Inc row: K10, m1, k14, m1, k10 (36 sts).
Inc row: K11, m1, k14, m1, k11 (38 sts).
Inc row: K12, m1, k14, m1, k12 (40 sts).
Beg with a purl row, rev stocking-st 11 rows.

Shape sides
Dec row: K2tog, k to last 2 sts, k2tog tbl.
Next row: Purl.
Rep last 2 rows 11 times more (16 sts).
Cast off.

Base

Using the thumb method and A, cast on 16 sts and work in rev stocking-st.
First row (RS): Purl.
Inc row: K1, m1, k to last st, m1, k1.
Rep first 2 rows 4 times more (26 sts).
Beg with a purl row, rev stocking-st 5 rows.
Dec row: K2tog, k to last 2 sts, k2tog tbl.
Next row: Purl.
Rep last 2 rows 4 times more (16 sts).
Cast off.

Head

Beg at centre back of head using the thumb method and A, cast on 9 sts and beg in rev stocking-st.
First and foll 5 alt rows (RS): Purl.
Inc row: K1, (m1, k1) to end (17 sts).
Inc row: K1, (m1, k2) to end (25 sts).
Inc row: K1, (m1, k3) to end (33 sts).
Inc row: K1, (m1, k4) to end (41 sts).
Inc row: K1, (m1, k5) to end (49 sts).
Inc row: K1, (m1, k6) to end (57 sts).
Beg with a purl row, rev stocking-st 13 rows.
Dec row: K5, (k2tog, k1) 16 times, k4 (41 sts).
Beg with a purl row, rev stocking-st 3 rows.
Dec row: K7, (k2tog, k3) 6 times, k4 (35 sts).
Cont in stocking-st.
Next row: (K1 tbl) to end.
Beg with a purl row, stocking-st 3 rows.
Dec row: (K3, k2tog) to end (28 sts).
Beg with a purl row, stocking-st 5 rows.
Dec row: (K2, k2tog) to end (21 sts).
Next and foll alt row: Purl.
Dec row: (K1, k2tog) to end (14 sts).
Dec row: (K2tog) to end (7 sts).
Thread yarn through sts on needle, pull tight and secure.

Hind legs (make 2)

Using the thumb method and A, cast on 30 sts and beg in rev stocking-st.
Beg with a purl row, rev stocking-st 11 rows.
Cont in stocking-st and beg with a purl row, stocking-st 7 rows.
Dec row (RS): (K1, k2tog) to end (20 sts).
Purl 1 row.
Dec row: (K2tog) to end (10 sts).
Thread yarn through sts on needle, pull tight and secure.

Forelegs (make 2)

Using the thumb method and A, cast on 20 sts and beg in rev stocking-st.
Beg with a purl row, rev stocking-st 19 rows.
Cont in stocking-st and beg with a purl row, stocking-st 7 rows.
Dec row (RS): (K2tog) to end (10 sts).
Thread yarn through sts on needle, pull tight and secure.

Horns (make 2)

Beg at base using the thumb method and B, cast on 15 sts.
Beg with a purl row, stocking-st 3 rows.
Shape horn
Row 1 (RS): K12, turn.
Row 2: S1p, p8, turn.
Row 3: S1k, k to end.
Row 4: Purl.
Row 5: Knit.
Row 6: Purl.
Rows 7 to 12: Rep rows 1 to 6 once.
Row 13: K2tog, k10, turn.
Row 14: S1p, p8, turn.
Row 15: S1k, k to last 2 sts, k2tog tbl (13 sts).
Row 16: Purl.
Row 17: Knit.
Row 18: Purl.
Row 19: K2tog, k8, turn.
Row 20: S1p, p6, turn.
Row 21: S1k, k to last 2 sts, k2tog tbl (11 sts).
Row 22: Purl.
Row 23: K2tog, k to last 2 sts, k2tog tbl.
Row 24: Purl.
Rows 25 and 26: As rows 23 and 24 (7 sts).
Row 27: K2tog, k to last 2 sts, k2tog tbl (5 sts).
Thread yarn through sts on needle, pull tight and secure.

Ears (make 2)

Beg at base using the thumb method and A, cast on 6 sts and work in stocking-st. Purl 1 row.

Inc row (RS): K1, (m1, k1) to end (11 sts). Beg with a purl row, stocking-st 5 rows.

Dec row: K2tog, (k1, k2tog) to end (7 sts). Thread yarn through sts on needle, pull tight and secure.

Tail

Beg at top edge using the thumb method and A, cast on 5 sts and work in rev stocking-st.

First and foll alt row (RS): Purl.

Inc row: K1, (m1, k1) to end (9 sts).

Inc row: K2, (m1, k1) to last st, k1 (15 sts). Beg with a purl row, rev stocking-st 9 rows.

Dec row: (K1, k2tog) to end (10 sts). Purl 1 row.

Dec row: (K2tog) to end 5 sts. Thread yarn through sts on needle, pull tight and secure.

Making up

Body

With reverse side of stocking stitch as the right side, place the two halves of body together matching all edges and join row ends. Stuff body leaving neck and lower edge open, filling out base with plenty of stuffing.

Base

Pin base to lower edge of body, noting that the reverse side of stocking stitch is the right side, and sew base to body leaving a gap. Adjust stuffing in base, adding more stuffing if needed, and close gap.

Head

Gather round cast-on stitches of head, pull tight and secure. Join row ends of head leaving a gap, stuff head, pushing stuffing into snout and top of head. Close gap and pin and sew head to body, adding more stuffing to body if needed.

Hind legs

Join row ends of hind legs and stuff. Place body on a flat surface and pin hind legs to body. Sew cast-on stitches of hind legs to body all the way round.

Forelegs

Join row ends of forelegs and stuff. With seam at centre of inside edge, oversew cast-on stitches. Sew forelegs to each side of body, sewing cast-off stitches to neck.

Horns

Join row ends of horns from tip, pushing in a little stuffing with tweezers or tip of scissors. Sew a running stitch along this seam and pull tight to curl horn and secure. Sew horns behind top of head and curl round to front and catch tip in place.

Ears

Join row ends of ears and with this seam at centre back, fold cast-on stitches in half and catch in place. Sew ears to sides of head below horns.

Tail

With reverse side of stocking stitch as the right side, gather round cast-on stitches of tail, pull tight and secure. Stuff tail and pin and sew outside edge to back of Ram above base.

Features

To make eyes, tie 2 knots in 2 lengths of dark brown yarn, winding the yarn round 6 times to make each knot (see page 120). Tie eyes to head with 5 clear knitted stitches in between and run ends into head. Embroider nose and mouth in dark brown using straight stitches as shown in picture. (See page 120 for how to begin and fasten off invisibly for the embroidery.)

Although the turkey originated in North and Central America, it was mistakenly named after what was believed to be its country of origin. Turkeys have great hearing, but no external ears. Their field of vision extends to 270 degrees, which means that they can see movement almost 100yd (90m) away. Wild turkeys can reach speeds of 55mph (88km/h) when in flight and can run at 25mph (40km/h).

TURKEY

Information you'll need

Finished size
Turkey measures 6in (15cm) in height

Materials
Any DK yarn:
50g black (A)
20g light brown (B)
20g white (C)
20g rustic red (D)
20g mustard (E)
Oddment of beige for beak (F)
Oddment of bright red for wattle (G)
Note: amounts are generous
but approximate
A pair of 3.25mm (US3:UK10) needles
Acrylic toy stuffing
Knitters' blunt-ended pins and
a knitters' needle for sewing up
Tweezers for stuffing small parts (optional)

Tension
26 sts x 34 rows measure 4in (10cm)
square over stocking-st using 3.25mm
needles and DK yarn before stuffing

Abbreviations
See page 123

turkey

How to make Turkey

Body

Beg at neck using the thumb method and A, cast on 20 sts.

First and foll 3 alt rows (WS): Purl.

Inc row: *K2, (m1, k2) 4 times; rep from * once (28 sts).

Inc row: *K4, (m1, k2) 4 times, k2; rep from * once (36 sts).

Inc row: *K6, (m1, k2) 4 times, k4; rep from * once (44 sts).

Inc row: *K8, (m1, k2) 4 times, k6; rep from * once (52 sts).

Beg with a purl row, stocking-st 29 rows.

Dec row: *K8, (k2tog) twice, k2, (k2tog) twice, k8; rep from * once (44 sts).

Next and foll 2 alt rows: Purl.

Dec row: *K6, (k2tog) twice, k2, (k2tog) twice, k6; rep from * once (36 sts).

Dec row: *K4, (k2tog) twice, k2, (k2tog) twice, k4; rep from * once (28 sts).

Dec row: *K2, (k2tog) twice, k2, (k2tog) twice, k2; rep from * once (20 sts).

Purl 1 row.

Cast off.

Feet (make 4 pieces)

Using the thumb method and E, cast on 8 sts.

Purl 1 row.

Inc row (RS): K1, (m1, k2) to last st, m1, k1 (12 sts).

Beg with a purl row, stocking-st 3 rows.

**Shape toes

Next row: K4, turn and work on these 4 sts.

Beg with a purl row, stocking-st 3 rows.

Dec row: K1, k2tog, k1 (3 sts).

Thread yarn through rem sts, pull tight and secure.**

With RS facing, rejoin yarn to sts on needle and rep from ** to ** twice.

Tail (make 2 pieces)

Beg at lower edge using the thumb method and A, cast on 12 sts.

Purl 1 row.

Join on and break off colours as required.

Work next 7 rows in A as foll:

Row 1 (RS): (Inc 1) to end (24 sts).

Row 2: Purl.

Row 3: Knit.

Row 4: Purl.

Row 5: *K1, (inc 1) twice, k1; rep from * 5 times more (36 sts).

Row 6: Purl.

Row 7: Knit.

Work next 8 rows in B as foll:

Row 8: Purl.

Row 9: *K2, (inc 1) twice, k2; rep from * 5 times more (48 sts).

Row 10: Purl.

Row 11: Knit.

Row 12: Purl.

Row 13: *K3, (inc 1) twice, k3; rep from * 5 times more (60 sts).

Row 14: Purl.

Row 15: Knit.

Work next 2 rows in A as foll:

Row 16: Purl.

Row 17: *K4, (inc 1) twice, k4; rep from * 5 times more (72 sts).

Work next 5 rows in C as foll:

Row 18: Purl.

Row 19: Knit.

Row 20: Purl.

Row 21: *K5, (inc 1) twice, k5; rep from * 5 times more (84 sts).

Row 22: Purl.

Cast off loosely.

Neck and head

Beg at lower edge using the thumb method and A, cast on 10 sts.

First and foll alt row (WS): Purl.

Inc row: K1, (m1, k1) to end (19 sts).

Inc row: K1, (m1, k2) to end (28 sts).

Beg with a purl row, stocking-st 7 rows.

Garter-st 2 rows.

Change to D and beg with a knit row, stocking-st 2 rows.

Shape next row: K2, m1, k9, k2tog, k2, k2tog, k9, m1, k2.

Beg with a purl row, stocking-st 15 rows.

Shape top of head

Dec row: (K2, k2tog) to end (21 sts).

Next and foll alt row: Purl.

Dec row: (K1, k2tog) to end (14 sts).

Dec row: (K2tog) to end (7 sts).

Thread yarn through sts on needle, pull tight and secure.

DID YOU KNOW?

Benjamin Franklin wanted to make the wild turkey the national bird of the United States rather than the bald eagle.

Wings (make 2)
Using the thumb method and A, cast on 16 sts.
Purl 1 row.
Inc row (RS): K1, (m1, k2) to last st, m1, k1 (24 sts).
Beg with a purl row, stocking-st 5 rows.
Dec row: K2tog, k to last 2 sts, k2tog.
Next row: Purl.
Rep last 2 rows 5 times more (12 sts).
Dec row: (K2tog) to end (6 sts).
Thread yarn through sts on needle, pull tight and secure.

Beak
Using the thumb method and F, cast on 8 sts.
Purl 1 row.
Dec row (RS): (K2tog) to end (4 sts).
Thread yarn through sts on needle, pull tight and secure.

Eye pieces (make 2)
Beg at top edge using the thumb method and E, cast on 4 sts.
Purl 1 row.
Inc row (RS): K1, m1, k2, m1, k1 (6 sts).
Beg with a purl row, stocking-st 3 rows.
Dec row: K1, (k2tog) twice, k1 (4 sts).
Beg with a purl row, stocking-st 3 rows.
Thread yarn through sts on needle, pull tight and secure.

Wattle
Beg at top edge using the thumb method and G, cast on 10 sts.
Beg with a purl row, stocking-st 5 rows.
Dec row: K1, (k2tog, k1) to end (7 sts).
Thread yarn through sts on needle, pull tight and secure.

Making up

Body
Join row ends of body leaving a gap. With this seam at centre of underneath side, join cast-on and cast-off stitches. Stuff body and close gap.

Feet
Place 2 pieces of feet together matching all edges and oversew on right side around toes. Stuff toes, pushing stuffing into toes with tweezers or tip of scissors. Stuff feet and join cast-on stitches. Place Turkey on a flat surface. Pin feet to body. Sew in place.

Tail
Place 2 pieces of tail together, matching all edges and join cast-off stitches. Lightly stuff keeping tail flat. Pin and sew lower edge of tail to body all the way round.

Neck and head
Gather round cast-on stitches of neck, pull tight and secure. Join row ends of head and neck leaving a gap, stuff and close gap. Sew black part of neck to body at centre front.

Wings
Fold cast-on stitches of wings in half and oversew. Join row ends of wings on right side. Pin wings to sides of Turkey and sew cast-on edge and approx 2in (5cm) down shaped side to body.

Beak
Join row ends of beak and sew beak to head all the way round.

Eye pieces
Place eye pieces either side of beak and sew in place round outside edge.

Wattle
Join row ends of wattle and with this seam at centre back, sew wattle beneath beak.

Features
To make eyes, tie 2 knots in 2 lengths of black yarn, winding the yarn round 6 times to make each knot (see page 120). Tie eyes to eye pieces at either side of beak and run ends into head.

turkey

Llamas are highly social animals with a keen sense of hearing, smell and sight. Their thick, incredibly soft coats also help llamas to thrive in extreme cold climates. Female llamas nuzzle and hum to their newborns. Llamas also hum when they are happy. Although they have even, docile temperaments, they have been known to spit when angered or feeling threatened, but that's mostly at each other.

LLAMA

DID YOU KNOW?
Llamas communicate with a series of ear, body and tail postures.

DID YOU KNOW?
Their long ears curve slightly inwards, similar in shape to a banana.

Information you'll need

Finished size
Llama measures 10in (25cm) in height

Materials
Any DK yarn:
80g golden cream (A)
10g fawn (B)
Oddment of black for features
Note: amounts are generous
but approximate
A pair of 3.25mm (US3:UK10) needles
Acrylic toy stuffing
Knitters' blunt-ended pins and a knitters'
needle for sewing up

Tension
26 sts x 34 rows measure 4in (10cm)
square over stocking-st using 3.25mm
needles and DK yarn before stuffing

Abbreviations
See page 123

How to make Llama

Body (make 2 pieces)

Beg at lower edge using the thumb method and A, cast on 28 sts and work in garter-st.

First and foll 3 alt rows (RS): Knit.
Inc row: K9, m1, k10, m1, k9 (30 sts).
Inc row: K10, m1, k10, m1, k10 (32 sts).
Inc row: K11, m1, k10, m1, k11 (34 sts).
Inc row: K12, m1, k10, m1, k12 (36 sts).
Garter-st 12 rows.
Dec row: K2tog, k to last 2 sts, k2tog tbl.
Next row: Knit.
Rep last 2 rows 8 times more (18 sts).
Dec row: K2tog, k to last 2 sts, k2tog tbl.
Garter-st 3 rows.
Rep last 4 rows once, then dec row once (12 sts).
Garter-st 24 rows, ending on a RS facing row.
Cast off in garter-st.

Base

Using the thumb method and A, cast on 14 sts and work in rev stocking-st.
First row (RS): Purl.
Inc row: K1, m1, k to last st, m1, k1.
Rep first 2 rows 4 times more (24 sts).
Beg with a purl row, rev stocking-st 5 rows.
Dec row: K2tog, k to last 2 sts, k2tog tbl.
Next row: Purl.
Rep last 2 rows 4 times more (14 sts).
Cast off.

Head

Beg at back of head using the thumb method and A, cast on 10 sts and beg in garter-st.
Inc row (RS): (K1, inc 1) to end (15 sts).
Next and foll 4 alt rows: Knit.
Inc row: (K2, inc 1) to end (20 sts).
Inc row: (K3, inc 1) to end (25 sts).
Inc row: (K4, inc 1) to end (30 sts).
Inc row: (K5, inc 1) to end (35 sts).
Inc row: (K6, inc 1) to end (40 sts).
Garter-st 15 rows.
Dec row: (K3, k2tog) to end (32 sts).
Next row: (K1 tbl) to end.
Cont in stocking-st and beg with a knit row, stocking-st 6 rows.
Dec row: (K2, k2tog) to end (24 sts).
Beg with a purl row, stocking-st 3 rows.
Dec row: (K1, k2tog) to end (16 sts).
Purl 1 row.
Dec row: (K2tog) to end (8 sts).
Thread yarn through sts on needle, pull tight and secure.

Hind legs (make 2)

Beg at top of leg using the thumb method and A, cast on 18 sts and beg in garter-st.
Garter-st 24 rows.
Change to B and knit 1 row.
Cont in rev stocking-st and beg with a knit row, rev stocking-st 6 rows.
Dec row (WS): (K2tog) to end (9 sts).
Thread yarn through sts on needle, pull tight and secure.

Forelegs (make 2)

Beg at shoulder using the thumb method and A, cast on 8 sts and beg in garter-st.
Inc row (RS): (Inc 1) to end (16 sts).
Garter-st 25 rows.
Change to B and knit 1 row.
Cont in rev stocking-st and beg with a knit row, rev stocking-st 6 rows.
Dec row: (K2tog) to end (8 sts).
Thread yarn through sts on needle, pull tight and secure.

Ears (make 2)

Beg at base using the thumb method and A, cast on 6 sts and work in stocking-st.
Purl 1 row.
Inc row (RS): (K1, m1, k1, m1, k1) twice (10 sts).
Beg with a purl row, stocking-st 7 rows.
Dec row: K2, k2tog, k2, k2og, k2 (8 sts).
Purl 1 row.
Dec row: (K1, k2tog, k1) twice (6 sts).
Thread yarn through sts on needle, pull tight and secure.

Tail

Beg at base of tail using the thumb method and A, cast on 4 sts and work in garter-st.
Inc row (RS): Inc k-wise into first and last st.
Next row: Knit.
Rep last 2 rows 3 times more (12 sts).
Garter-st 4 rows.
Dec row: (K1, k2tog) to end (8 sts).
Knit 1 row.
Dec row: (K2tog) to end (4 sts).
Thread yarn through sts on needle, pull tight and secure.

Making up

Body

Place the two halves of body together matching all edges and join row ends. Stuff body and neck leaving neck and lower edge open, filling out base with plenty of stuffing.

Base

Pin base to lower edge of body, noting that the reverse side of stocking stitch is the right side, and sew base to body leaving a gap. Adjust stuffing in base, adding more stuffing if needed, and close gap.

Head

Gather round cast-on stitches, pull tight and secure. Join row ends of head by oversewing on right side leaving a gap, stuff and close gap. Pin and sew head to Llama, adding more stuffing to neck if needed.

Hind legs

Oversewing row ends on right side, join row ends of hind legs and hooves and stuff. Place body on a flat surface and pin and sew cast-on stitches of hind legs to body all the way round.

Forelegs

Gather round cast-on stitches, pull tight and secure. Oversew row ends on right side, join row ends of forelegs and hooves leaving a gap, stuff and close gap. Sew forelegs to body at shoulders, approx 2in (5cm) down from head.

Ears

With right sides of stocking stitch outside, fold ears in half and join row ends. Sew ears to head.

Tail

Join straight row ends of tail and stuff. Sew base of tail to body at centre back, all the way round.

Features

To make eyes, tie 2 knots in 2 lengths of black yarn, winding the yarn round 6 times to make each knot (see page 120). Tie eyes to head with 5 clear knitted stitches in between and run ends into head. Embroider nose and mouth in black, embroidering 2 horizontal stitches close together for nose and straight stitches for mouth. Embroider a horizontal eyelash at the back of each eye, as shown in the picture. (See page 120 for how to begin and fasten off invisibly for the embroidery.)

llama

Donkeys are very affectionate animals and enjoy companionship. Their favourite pastime is rolling in the dust. Miniature donkeys can be as small as 36in (91cm), while mammoth donkeys can measure over 54in (137cm). In southern Spain there is a giant, pure breed of donkey called the Andalucian-Cordobesan, which is as big as a racehorse! Large donkeys are often used as security guards for herds of cattle or sheep.

DONKEY

DID YOU KNOW?
A donkey's eyes are placed so that it is able to see all four of its feet no matter which way it looks.

Information you'll need

Finished size
Donkey measures 10in (25cm) in height

Materials
Any DK yarn:
80g grey (A)
20g white (B)
40g black (C)
Oddment of dusky pink for features
Note: amounts are generous but
approximate
A pair of 3.25mm (US3:UK10) needles
Acrylic toy stuffing
Knitters' blunt-ended pins and a knitters'
needle for sewing up

Tension
26 sts x 34 rows measure 4in (10cm)
square over stocking-st using 3.25mm
needles and DK yarn before stuffing

Abbreviations
See page 123
Special abbreviation: Loop-st
Insert RH needle into next st, place first
finger of LH behind LH needle and wind
yarn clockwise round needle and finger
twice, then just round needle once. Knit
this st, pulling 3 loops through. Place loops
just made onto LH needle and knit into
the back of them. Pull loops just made
sharply down to secure. Cont to next st.

How to make Donkey

Body (make 2 pieces)

Beg at lower edge using the thumb method and A, cast on 32 sts.

First and foll 3 alt rows (WS): Purl.

Inc row: K9, m1, k14, m1, k9 (34 sts).

Inc row: K10, m1, k14, m1, k10 (36 sts).

Inc row: K11, m1, k14, m1, k11 (38 sts).

Inc row: K12, m1, k14, m1, k12 (40 sts).

Beg with a purl row, stocking-st 11 rows.

Shape sides

Dec row: K2tog, k to last 2 sts, k2tog tbl.

Next row: Purl.

Rep last 2 rows 11 times more (16 sts).

Cast off.

Base

Using the thumb method and A, cast on 16 sts.

First row (WS): Purl.

Inc row: K1, m1, k to last st, m1, k1.

Rep first 2 rows 4 times more (26 sts).

Beg with a purl row, stocking-st 5 rows.

Dec row: K2tog, k to last 2 sts, k2tog tbl.

Next row: Purl.

Rep last 2 rows 4 times more (16 sts).

Cast off.

Head

Beg at centre back of head using the thumb method and A, cast on 9 sts.

First and foll 5 alt rows (WS): Purl.

Inc row: K1, (m1, k1) to end (17 sts).

Inc row: K1, (m1, k2) to end (25 sts).

Inc row: K1, (m1, k3) to end (33 sts).

Inc row: K1, (m1, k4) to end (41 sts).

Inc row: K1, (m1, k5) to end (49 sts).

Inc row: K1, (m1, k6) to end (57 sts).

Beg with a purl row, stocking-st 13 rows.

Dec row: K14, (k2tog, k1) 10 times, k13 (47 sts).

Beg with a purl row, stocking-st 3 rows.

Dec row: K12, (k2tog, k1) 8 times, k11 (39 sts).

Purl 1 row.

Change to B.

Next row: (K1 tbl) to end.

Purl 1 row.

Dec row: K2tog, k to last 2 sts, k2tog tbl.

Next row: Purl.

Rep last 2 rows twice (33 sts).

Dec row: K5, (k2tog) 4 times, k7, (k2tog) 4 times, k5 (25 sts).

Purl 1 row.

Dec row: K5, (k2tog) twice, k7, (k2tog) twice, k5 (21 sts).

Cast off p-wise.

Hind legs (make 2)

Beg at hoof using the thumb method and C, cast on 11 sts.

First and foll alt row (WS): Purl.

Inc row: K3, (m1, k1) 6 times, k2 (17 sts).

Inc row: K5, (m1, k1) 8 times, k4 (25 sts).

Beg with a purl row, stocking-st 9 rows.

Change to A and dec.

Dec row: K4, (k2tog, k1) 6 times, k3 (19 sts).

Beg with a purl row, stocking-st 17 rows.

Cast off.

Forelegs (make 2)

Beg at hoof using the thumb method C, cast on 8 sts.

First and foll alt row (WS): Purl.

Inc row: K1, (m1, k1) to end (15 sts).

Inc row: K1, (m1, k2) to end (22 sts).

Beg with a purl row, stocking-st 7 rows.

Change to A and dec.

Dec row: K1, (k2tog, k1) to end (15 sts).

Beg with a purl row, stocking-st 23 rows.

Dec row: (K1, k2tog) to end (10 sts).

Thread yarn through sts on needle, pull tight and secure.

Ears (make 2)

Beg at lower edge using the thumb method and A, cast on 12 sts.

Purl 1 row.

Inc row (RS): K1, (m1, k2) to last st, m1, k1 (18 sts).

Beg with a purl row, stocking-st 9 rows.

Dec row: K2, (k2tog) 3 times, k2, (k2tog) 3 times, k2 (12 sts).

Dec row: (P2tog) to end (6 sts).

Thread yarn though sts on needle, pull tight and secure.

Mane

Using the thumb method and C, cast on 35 sts loosely.

First row: (Loop-st) to end.

Cast off loosely k-wise.

Tail

Beg at one end using the thumb method and A, cast on 8 sts.

Beg with a purl row, stocking-st 15 rows.

Cast off.

Making up

Body

Place the two halves of body together matching all edges and join row ends. Stuff body leaving neck and lower edge open, filling out base with plenty of stuffing.

Base

Pin base to lower edge of body and sew base to body, leaving a gap. Adjust stuffing in base, adding more stuffing if needed, and close gap.

Head

Join row ends of muzzle and with this seam at centre of underneath side, join cast-off stitches. Gather round cast-on stitches, pull tight and secure. Join row ends of head leaving a gap, stuff, pushing stuffing into muzzle and top of head and close gap. Pin and sew head to body, adding more stuffing to body if needed.

Hind legs

Gather round cast-on stitches of hind legs, pull tight and secure. Join row ends of hind legs and stuff, pushing a ball of stuffing into hoof. Place body on a flat surface and pin hind legs to body. Sew cast-off stitches of hind legs to body all the way round.

Forelegs

Gather round cast-on stitches of forelegs, pull tight and secure. Join row ends leaving a gap, stuff and close gap. Sew forelegs to each side of body, sewing stitches pulled tight on a thread to neck.

Ears

Join row ends of ears and with this seam at centre front, fold lower edge of each ear in half and catch in place. Sew ears to top of head.

Mane

Fold mane in half, oversew and sew lower edge of mane to head between ears and down back of head.

Tail

Make a tassel in black yarn 1in (2.5cm) long (see page 121). Anchor tassel to inside edge of one end of tail. Join row ends of tail on right side using mattress stitch (see page 118). Sew tail to body and trim ends of tassel.

Features

To make eyes, tie 2 knots in 2 lengths of black yarn, winding the yarn round 6 times to make each knot (see page 120). Tie eyes to row above muzzle with 5 clear knitted stitches in between and run ends into head. Work nostrils in the same way using dusky pink and winding the yarn round 4 times to make each knot. Tie nostrils to muzzle with 7 clear knitted stitches in between.

donkey

WOULD CATS ENJOY KNITTING CLASSES?

How long does it take a goat to grow a goatee?

How do roosters get up so early every morning?

Where does a Highland bull go to get his fringe cut?

Techniques

Getting started

Buying yarn

All the patterns in this book are worked in double knitting (or light worsted in the US). There are many DK yarns on the market, from natural fibres to acrylic blends. Acrylic yarn is a good choice as it washes without shrinking, but always follow the care instructions on the ball band. Be cautious about using a brushed or mohair-type yarn if the toy is intended for a baby or very young child as the fibres can be swallowed.

Tension

Tension is not critical when knitting toys if the right yarn and needles are used. All the toys in this book are knitted on 3.25mm (US3:UK10) knitting needles. This should turn out at approximately 26 stitches and 34 rows over 4in (10cm) square. If using more than one colour in the design, it is advisable to use the same type of yarn as described on the ball band as some yarns are bulkier and will produce fabric that is slightly bigger.

Slip knot

1 Leave a long length of yarn – as a rough guide, allow ⅜in (1cm) for each stitch to be cast on plus an extra length for sewing up. Wind the yarn from the ball round your left index finger from front to back and then to back again. Slide loop from finger and pull new loop through from the centre and place this loop from back to front on to the needle that is in your right hand.

2 Pull the tail of yarn down to tighten the knot slightly and pull the yarn from the ball to form a loose loop.

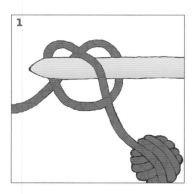

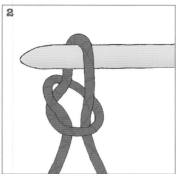

Casting on

Thumb method

1 Make a slip knot. Hold the needle in your right hand with your index finger on the slip knot loop to keep it in place.

2 Wrap the loose tail end round the left thumb, from front to back. Push the needle point through the thumb loop from front to back. Wind the ball end of yarn round the needle from left to right.

3 Pull the loop through the thumb loop, then remove your thumb. Gently pull the new loop tight using the tail yarn.

4 Repeat until the desired number of stitches are on the needle.

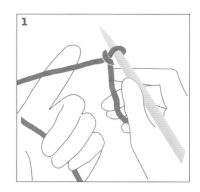

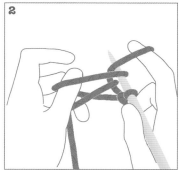

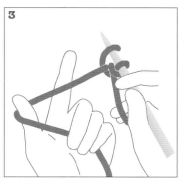

Cable method

When casting on part way through knitting, such as for the hole for the Pig's tail, a two-needle method, such as the cable method, is used:

1 Work along row to the point where cast-on stitches are to be placed. Turn work. Insert the right-hand needle from front to back between the first and second stitch on the left-hand needle and wrap yarn round tip of right-hand needle from back to front.

2 Slide the right-hand needle through to the front to catch the new loop of yarn.

3 Place the new loop of yarn onto the left-hand needle, inserting the left-hand needle from front to back.

4 Repeat this until you have the required number of cast-on stitches.

5 Turn work once again and continue along row.

113

Knit stitch

1 Hold the needle with the cast-on stitches in your left hand. Place the tip of the empty right-hand needle into the first stitch on the left-hand needle from right to left. Wrap the yarn anti-clockwise around the tip of the right-hand needle.

2 Pull the yarn through to create a new loop.

3 Slip the loop off the left-hand needle with the new stitch on the right-hand needle. Continue in the same way for each stitch on the left-hand needle. To start a new row, turn your work to swap the needles and repeat these instructions.

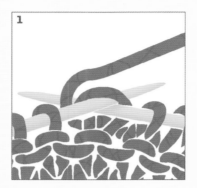

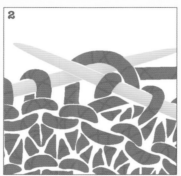

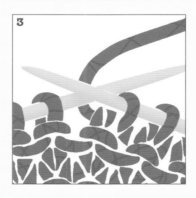

Purl stitch

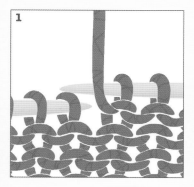
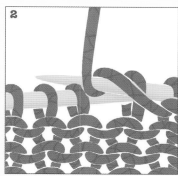
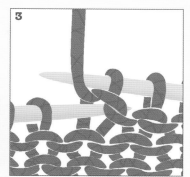

1 Hold the yarn at the front of the work as shown.

2 Place the right-hand needle into the first stitch from front to back. Wrap the yarn anti-clockwise around the tip of the right-hand needle.

3 Bring the right-hand needle back through the stitch to create a new loop. Slip loop off left-hand needle with the new loop on right-hand needle.

Types of stitch

Garter stitch (A)
Knit every row.

Stocking stitch (B)
Knit on the right side and purl on the wrong side.

Reverse stocking stitch (C)
Purl on the right side and knit on the wrong side.

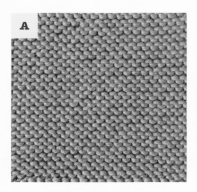

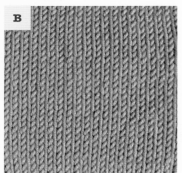

Increasing

Two methods are used in this book for increasing the number of stitches: inc and m1.

Inc – Knit twice into the next stitch. To do this on a knit row, simply knit into the next stitch but do not slip it off. Take the point of the right-hand needle around and knit again into the back of the stitch before removing the loop from the left-hand needle.

To do this on a purl row, purl first into the back of the stitch but do not slip it off. Purl again into the front of the stitch before removing the loop from the left-hand needle. You have now made two stitches out of one.

M1 – Make a stitch by picking up the horizontal loop between the needles and placing it on to the left-hand needle. Now knit into the back of it to twist it, or purl into the back of it on a purl row.

Decreasing

To decrease a stitch, simply knit two stitches together to make one stitch out of the two stitches, or if the instructions say k3tog, then knit three stitches together to make one out of the three stitches. To get a neat appearance to your finished work, this is done as follows:

At the beginning of a knit row and throughout the row, k2tog by knitting two stitches together through the front of the loops.

At the end of a knit row, if these are the very last two stitches in the row, then knit together through back of loops.

At the beginning of a purl row, if these are the very first stitches in the row, then purl together through back of loops. Purl two together along the rest of the row through the front of the loops.

Casting off

1 Knit two stitches on to the right-hand needle, then slip the first stitch over the second and let it drop off the needle. One stitch is remaining.

2 Knit another stitch so you have two stitches on the right-hand needle again.

3 Repeat the process until only one stitch is left on the left-hand needle. Break yarn and thread it through the remaining stitch.

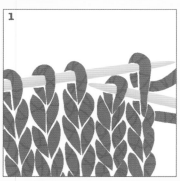

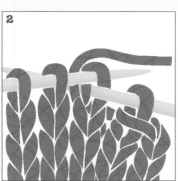

Sewing up

The animals in this book are put together using simple sewing techniques.

Join row ends

Pieces can be joined by oversewing on the wrong side and turning the piece the right side out. For smaller pieces or pieces that cannot be turned, oversew on the right side.

Join striped row ends

Join row ends on the body of Cat by sewing back and forth one stitch in from the edge on the wrong side.

Mattress stitch

Join row ends of Donkey's tail using mattress stitch by taking small straight stitches back and forth on the right side of work (see diagram above right).

Backstitch

Sew round outside edge of Cow's patches and Hen's eye pieces using backstitch. Bring the needle out at the start of the stitch line, take a small stitch, bringing the needle out a bit further along. Insert the needle at the end of the first stitch and bring it out still further along. Continue in the same way to create a line of stitches.

Threading yarn through stitches

Sometimes the instructions say: thread yarn through stitches on needle, pull tight and secure. To do this, break the yarn, leaving a long end, and thread a knitters' needle with this end. Now pass the knitters' needle through all the stitches on the knitting needle, slipping each stitch off the knitting needle in turn. Draw yarn through stitches. To secure, pass the knitters' needle once again through all the stitches in a complete circle and pull tight.

Placing a marker

When placing a marker on the cast-on edge, as for the cow's muzzle, thread a knitters' needle with yarn in a contrasting colour and count the number of stitches to where the marker is to be placed. Pass the knitters' needle between these stitches and tie a loose loop around the cast-on edge with a double knot and trim ends.

Embroidery

To begin embroidery invisibly, tie a knot in the end of the yarn. Take a large stitch through the work, coming up to begin the embroidery. Allow the knot to disappear through the knitting and be caught in the stuffing. To fasten off invisibly, sew a few stitches back and forth through the work, inserting the needle where the yarn comes out.

Nose and mouth

Embroider some features, such as the nose and mouth of the cat and dog, using straight stitches.

Eyes

1 Make a loose single slip knot and then wind the yarn around five more times, making a total of six times, or the number of times stated in the pattern. (The diagram on the right shows the yarn being wound three more times.) Pull the knot tight.

2 You now have an oval-shaped eye. Make two and check that the knots are the same size. Tie eyes to head in position as stated in the instructions. Run ends into head.

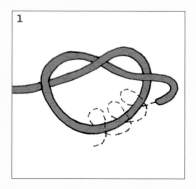

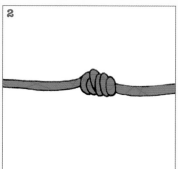

Make a twisted cord

A twisted cord is used for the tails of the cow, pig and highland bull.

1 Cut even strands of yarn to the number and length stated in the pattern and knot each end. Anchor one end, e.g. tie it to a door handle or chair, or ask a friend to hold it.

2 Take the other end and twist until it is tightly wound.

3 Hold the centre of the cord and place two ends together. Release the centre, so the two halves twist together. Smooth it out and knot ends together.

Making tassels

1 Take a piece of stiff card with a width that is the same as the length of the intended finished tassel plus 2in (5cm), and wrap yarn around it several times. Secure this bundle with a separate length of yarn threaded through at one end, leaving long ends, then cut the bundle at the opposite edge.

2 Keeping the bundle folded in half, wind a separate length of yarn a few times round the whole bundle, including the long ends of the tie, approx ½in (2cm) below the fold, to form the head of the tassel. Tie the two ends of this length of yarn together tightly. Trim all the ends of yarn at the base of the tassel to give a tidy finish. If you want a bushier tassel, unroll and separate the strands of yarn.

Stuffing and care

Spend a little time stuffing your toy evenly. Acrylic toy stuffing is ideal and plenty should be used, but not so much that it stretches the knitting and the stuffing can be seen through the stitches. Fill out any base, keeping it flat. Tweezers are useful for stuffing small parts.

Washable filling is recommended for all the stuffed toys so that you can hand-wash them in a non-biological detergent. Do not spin or tumble dry, but gently squeeze the excess water out, arrange the animal into its original shape and leave to dry.

Abbreviations

alt	alternate
approx	approximate
beg	begin(ning)
cm	centimetres
cont	continue
dec	decrease
DK	double knitting
foll	follow(ing)(s)
g	grams
garter-st	garter-stitch: knit every row
in	inch(es)
inc	increase
k	knit
k2tog	knit two stitches together: if these are the very last in the row, then work together through back of loops
k3tog	knit three stitches together
k-wise	knit ways
LH	left hand
m1	make one stitch: pick up horizontal loop between the needles and work into the back of it
mm	millimetres

p	purl
p2tog	purl two stitches together: if these stitches are the very first in the row, then work together through back of loops
p3tog	purl three stitches together
patt	pattern
p-wise	purl ways
rem	remain(ing)
rep	repeat
rev stocking-st	reverse stocking stitch: purl on the right side, knit on the wrong side
RH	right hand
RS	right side
slk	slip one stitch knit ways
slp	slip one stitch purl ways
st(s)	stitch(es)
stocking-st	stocking stitch: knit on the right side, purl on the wrong side
tbl	through back of loop(s)
tog	together
WS	wrong side
yb	yarn back
yrn	yarn round needle
( )	repeat instructions between brackets as many times as instructed

Conversions

Suppliers

Knitting needles

UK:	Metric:	US:
14	2mm	0
13	2.25mm	1
12	2.75mm	2
11	3mm	–
10	3.25mm	3
–	3.5mm	4
9	3.75mm	5
8	4mm	6
7	4.5mm	7
6	5mm	8
5	5.5mm	9
4	6mm	10
3	6.5mm	10.5
2	7mm	10.5
1	7.5mm	11
0	8mm	13
000	10mm	15

Yarn weight

UK:	US:
Double knitting	Light worsted

Terms

UK:	US:
Anti-clockwise	Counter-clockwise
Cast off	Bind off
Stocking stitch	Stockinette stitch
Tension	Gauge
Yarn round needle	Yarn over

Sirdar
www.sirdar.co.uk
+44 (0)1924 371 501

Stylecraft
www.stylecraft-yarns.co.uk
+44 (0)1535 609798

About the author

Sarah Keen was born and brought up in Wales in the UK. She discovered a love of knitting at a very early age: her mother taught her to knit when she was just four years old and by the age of nine she was making jackets and jumpers.

Sarah now works as a freelance pattern designer and finds calculating rows and stitches challenging but fascinating. She is experienced in designing knitted toys for children, having made several for her nephews and nieces. She also enjoys writing patterns for charity and publishes them at home. Sarah is passionate about knitting, finding it relaxing and therapeutic. This is her second book, following the success of her first, *Knitted Wild Animals,* which is also published by GMC Publications.

Acknowledgements

Thanks to Clare Wools, Aberystwyth, Wales for stocking many of the lovely yarns (*www.clarewools.co.uk*).

Special thanks to Alison and all supporting friends throughout the designing of this book.

Thanks to all the team at GMC Publications.

Index

index

To place an order, or to request a catalogue, contact:
GMC Publications Ltd
Castle Place, 166 High Street, Lewes, East Sussex, BN7 1XU
United Kingdom
Tel: +44 (0)1273 488005
www.gmcbooks.com